The Psyc

Me

The Extreme Ghost Hunter

By

Paul Green

and

Stephen Lambert

Mandrake

Published by
Mandrake of Oxford
PO Box 250
OXFORD
OX1 1AP (UK)

A CIP catalogue record for this book is available from the
British Library and the US Library of Congress.

978-1-906958-20-6

EXTREME
ghost
hunting

Published by

Cauliay Publishing & Distribution

PO Box 12076

Aberdeen

AB16 9AL

www.cauliaybooks.com

First Edition

ISBN 978-0-9568810-0-7

ACKNOWLEDGMENTS

PAUL GREEN

To my wife Susan, for her help, support and putting up with my tantrums during the writing of this book as well as her proof reading.

Thanks to my grown up children Michael and Kim. Both who read my first attempts and were supportive of my efforts. Finally to my beautiful granddaughter Sophie who helped granddad laugh and have fun when he was struggling to see the big picture.

A copy of this book will be kept for her to read when she is old enough and with luck I will be able to laugh with her then as well.

STEPHEN LAMBERT

Many thanks must go to my parents, Evan, Amy and friends who have given me great support over the years.

A big thank you must also go to all the locations who have allowed us to stay and carry out our research. My thanks also to Michael Molden for giving us the chance to publish this work.

Lastly my thoughts and love go out to Thomas Stanley Hall, a granddad who has helped me in this world and from the spirit world, you are sorely missed.

CONTENTS

FOREWORD

BY JASON KARL

Jason Karl is a TV presenter, ghost hunter and scare entertainment producer, and has presented countless programmes about the paranormal all over the world. Over the past decade he has travelled extensively in search of the supernatural and now runs the UK's biggest live scare entertainment company AtmosFEAR! Entertainment Group. You can find out more at www.jasondexterkarl.com.

In a world now over-saturated with books, films and TV shows covering the subject of ghosts and the supernatural, it is refreshing to see a work focusing not just on the well known 'haunts', but on the practical, and recent, investigations of some lesser known places.

'Extreme' ghost hunter Stephen Lambert, and his partner-in-haunting, the 'Psychic Biker', have undertaken the unenviable task of spending many days and nights searching for something which, for the most of us, is not part of everyday life experience.

Having spent many years as a ghost hunter myself, I know how tedious such investigations can be, so why do we do it at all? Because sometimes, very occasionally, something strange happens in these, often remote and forgotten, places which science is unable to explain.

These fleeting glimpses of the fantastical are the reward for the dedication of those that walk on the wild side of the supernatural realm, and in this book you will discover some of the truly remarkable encounters this brave pair have enjoyed/endured?

I am often asked if ghosts are scary? Can they harm you? - there is no short answer to this question, but as with anything we do not understand, it is wise to approach such things with caution, and take advice from those who have done it before - as this pair have.

Paul is a working medium, which means he can communicate with beings we cannot see. In this book he lets us into his case files, where he has come face to face with spirits haunting and terrifying, families in their own homes. Indeed he seems able to help move these spirits on, bringing peace to those that occupy these haunted houses, a rare gift, or as many mediums say - a curse?

I have spent time with Stephen and Paul investigating a well known haunted hotel, The Schooner Inn, and while it was not the most fruitful investigation in terms of paranormal activity, it was a pleasure to 'work' with them, and I wish them well with their ongoing research for truth - wherever it may take them...

Jason Dexter Karl

TV Presenter, Author

www.jasondexterkarl.com

THE PSYCHIC BIKER

Well, I guess one of the first questions I should answer is the name, "The Psychic Biker."

As with so much of my life it came about while in a pub with my bike club mates. A stranger must have been listening to our conversation and when I went to the bar she asked if I was really a psychic medium. This is a question I am used to being asked as I am 6 feet tall, (I have no idea what that is in metric, if you're that interested go look it up) heavily tattooed, have a shaven head and I am told that even in a good mood, a face that looks like a bulldog chewing a wasp.

So she got the usual spiel I give to people who ask that question and having been served I sat down. As the lady was leaving she made her goodbyes including to me and came out with the phrase "The Psychic Biker."

The name stuck and I decided to use it when I set up as a professional medium. How did I arrive at this stage in my life as medium and a ghost hunter? I am hardly someone with a background that would have led me down this path.

It all started when I was quite young but to be honest I just thought it was normal or as my mother said: "I had an over active imagination." The sort of thing I mean is when aged about 7/8 years I was on a school trips to castles/halls I would start trotting out information about the place after I touched the walls. Sad thing was seeing the gleam in my teacher's eye when he assumed I had an interest in history, maybe I should have told him how I really knew the information.

Around the same age, after my grandfather died in an institution I had quite a chat with him in my bedroom before the police arrived to tell my Nan he had died, back then that was how people were told as not many people had home phones.

Even in my early teens at school I was an oddball kid, yep I was the kid your mother told you not to play with. I was an avid reader and used to devour books on UFOs, magic, the occult and almost anything "off the wall".

I was more than happy with my own company and In fact at times I preferred it. After all I always had books or the spirit people to keep me company. I had a couple of mates but was never going to be one of the cool, kids, I guess that would describe many people's school days.

Oddly, given my interests and experiences in my youth when I hit my late teens I became a complete and utter cynic; Very much a "when you're dead your worm food" attitude. When my wife and her friend visited the local spiritualist church now and then I was very scathing in my comments.

I might have stayed in that sort of mode had there not been a huge change in my life in my late 40s when I gave up work to become a carer for my wife. That meant going from working away from home on oil rigs, usually working 90 hours a week to being at home with a huge drop in income and not working 90 hours a week, or at least not in the same hard physical manner. Maybe quite understandably I became quite stressed so it was suggested that I should try meditation.

It was probably my wife who suggested it; she wanted some peace I suspect. I was of course sceptical but was ready to try anything. So after a little research on how to meditate I gave it a go. As anyone who has tried this you will know it is not easy, either you end up drifting off and wondering what to have for dinner or you fall asleep. I was intrigued so stuck at it and from that start I began to wonder about the strange images, smells, sounds and in particular a picture of one man I kept getting in my head. Who I much later found out was my spirit guide

So I started to dig around on the internet and visit the library to start researching to find a reason for all this. Over about 18 months I had started to glean quite a bit of knowledge on medium ship and psychics but still scoffed at all that rubbish. I had also come across lots of info on how mediums and psychic faked things so I was still pretty much on the sceptical side of the fence.

Moving on from my reading and research I felt my next step was to visit a spiritualist church and see how things went "eyes on" so to speak, even though I vowed I was not going to sing along to the hymns. First church I went to was the church my wife had visited and the irony was not lost on me. I received a friendly and enthusiastic welcome, later I was to learn that is not always the case at all churches. I was still strictly an observer watching and trying to figure out how the mediums "did it".

Often I would bristle when even with what I considered limited knowledge I heard some mediums trot out information that was so general in nature I suspect that many parts of it could strike a chord with anyone. There were however still mediums that I could not "catch out." MY logical brain could not figure out how they "did it."

I then decided to broaden my experience and visit some other churches along with a fellow bike club member and good friend Wendy. That was fun as she is also biker and some mediums made the assumption we were together as a couple, other than as friends I mean of course; they would then come up with some outlandish readings and comments about our relationship as a couple.

Also there was always someone that one of us supposedly knew that had died on a motorcycle. We knew no one who has died on a bike and we weren't, as I said, a couple. Once again there though were other mediums that seemed to know information about myself that they shouldn't logically be able to know.

As a result of all this research and experiences which was spread over about 12 months I decided to give this mediumship game a go; always being of the opinion that if you want to fully understand something then it is best to try it for yourself.

So I continued to research deeper and practice what I learned. Looked again to the web and also books on topics such as "protection and opening up," in other words the basics of mediumship. This included how mediums work, how they receive messages, their sprit guides etc. All this with a very sceptical mind I must say.

The next step I felt was to attend an, "Open Circle." This is usually at a church where the public and trainee mediums could come along and under the guidance of an experienced medium, practice receiving and, passing messages from dead loved ones to other people in the circle without the stress of doing it live so to speak. Even then I was more of an observer, still trying to suss out this mediumship lark. Gradually I started to realize that some of the images and sensations I was "getting" but saying nothing about in the circle another person would then stand up and say.

What I found fascinating was that it was not general information which could be for almost anyone, (I had seen that done in churches as I have mentioned before). An example would be one time when I am getting mental images of underground pipes and staying quiet for fear of looking a real idiot, then a braver person stood up and described the same picture. That was odd in itself I thought, then when a member of the circle tells of her nightmare week with her garden having to be dug up due to a sewage pipe leak I was really struggling to come up with a reason other than mediumship/psychic ability, to explain it.

I could of course have assumed it was some plot to hoax myself and the rest of the circle or they had chatted before and the incident had been mentioned, I accept that. After all that's what ardent sceptics always say now to explain anything that could be termed accurate information from a medium. What I couldn't explain was my involvement, the fact that I had "seen" these images.

When the rest of the information was very specific about a deceased loved one I really was stuck for an explanation. I am now 100% discounting a clever scam to fool 7 people in the circle for the monetary gain of the £1 donation at the door that may be a sceptic's theory.

Trying to understand this I dug yet again deeper into the subject, both by more reading and participating in debates via on line forums including some ardent sceptical ones where I grew to know what the sacrificial lamb feels like, but also by practicing new techniques both alone and in churches.

As with most things I found that the more I practiced the better I became, plus I was learning a huge amount from watching other mediums, both what to do and what not to do in terms of how to deliver a message in the best possible way so it could be understood.

It sounds easy but that is one of the main skills of a medium. Learning to understand how the spirit world will use your senses to get info to you and give you the best possible chance of passing it accurately to the person you are reading for. My way of working I learnt was to first get the mental picture of the person who was deceased and then once the connection had been made more information came through.

Again this sounds easy but you try describing someone from a picture only you can see to someone who does know this person but it could have been a relative, friend or a school chum. Couldn't have made it easy and reversed that process could they the spirit world, oh no. I do feel that spirit use the mediums own personality and strengths when trying to pass info across though, therefore as I am and have always been a very visual person, finding it hard to absorb info through facts and figures unless I had some sort of visual representations to build on so again it is logical that the spirit world would choose to use that method to communicate with me. You will see that I am still looking for logic even among mediumship.

I also learnt how NOT to do readings, seeing the arrogance of some mediums who while getting a "no" response from information they were trying to pass on would tell that person it was their fault, "they were blocked." Even then at a pretty early stage of my development I vowed never to use that sort of tactic and be honest.

If I was struggling with giving a reading sometimes it was simply down to having a bad day, or having something else on my mind. Mediums are human and just as you can have a day when nothing you try to do goes right so can we. So at times, well only twice so far, I have simply apologized and told the person I was reading I couldn't read for them, my fault not theirs. I have always been acutely aware of the trust people place in mediums and take my responsibility to give 110% effort to getting that message over to them accurately from their loved ones very seriously.

Most of the time now though the information was flying in so fast it was hard to keep up and it was accurate and unique. For the sceptics who doubt that they tell me that Bartholomew is a common name. That was one of the oddest names I had to deliver and not I hope you would agree "common."

From visiting local churches and oddly my local pub I got to know a lady called Helen, no doubt when she reads that she will have a giggle at "lady". She was part of a development circle run by the woman who became my teacher, Linda. Long and short of it all is I was invited into a development circle by Linda. That in itself was a great honour and responsibility. You do not simply join a circle, you have to be invited and by joining you are making a commitment to your teacher, your fellow classmates, yourself and more importantly to the spirit world that says you will be there every week ready to work with them and for them no matter what. Linda I soon realised was one of the most honest, open and spiritual people I knew and that remains the case today.

My first night at the circle literally blew me away, at the end I was swaying with the energy in that circle. Over the time I was part of the circle I learnt so much, was told I had a great potential as a trance medium but never took that any further. Trance is where you allow a spirit person to use your body to communicate; again logically it makes sense to cut out the weak link, the medium and simply take control of, for example the

13

mediums voice. Me being me I could never voluntarily give up that degree of control.

I lost my reluctance in getting to my feet and speaking in front of people; I got used to passing on messages and had my first experience of transfiguration. Transfiguration is when the face and/or the body of the medium takes on the visage of the spirit person that is trying to communicate. The background to the whole tale is long and involved, if you ever meet me ask and I may tell you it, but the end result was to find myself on my feet seeing 6 very shocked faces staring back at me and total silence around the circle. Later I was told I stood up shouting angrily at two women who were giggling and my face and head changed into a much older men with a thin face with a black thin beard. To be honest I could not and cannot recall that part of that experience.

Despite all this research, practice and development across all the areas I have mentioned, which spanned about 6 years, I still didn't count myself as a medium, I always said I was "in development". An ongoing project shall we say, however after sometime within the circle I decided to move on. This was partly due to another member of the circle, a male, whose smutty comments about the women in the circle I hated and I knew I would end up losing my temper with him but also as the teachings were now angled to working the platform in the church. Something I had no real interest in doing. In fact, I have some reservation about the many religious aspects of spiritualism. So I ventured out into the big wide world of mediumship alone.

I still spent a lot of time in practice and research and after a while started to give readings outside the church, to friends and family. One of the first I did was for a fellow bike club member, who will remain nameless; I had known this guy for well over 10 years and was a bit doubtful about what I would be passed from spirit through me that I didn't already know. As a result of that reading I discovered from his deceased father coming through,

14

of his abusive childhood, something he had never mentioned to me or anyone else and the reason he shall remain nameless.

Things like that added to my growing list of episodes I could not explain to my still sceptical mind, yes a medium who is also a sceptic, told you I was an odd ball. I was again ready to expand my experience as a medium and while I continued to do readings I also wanted to try other "stuff."

I would guess anyone who is reading this will have some knowledge of the TV programme "Most Haunted." I watched this at times and the whole concept of how the medium working reminded me of my experiences as a kid visiting the castles on school trips. In fact that programme sparked an explosion in interest in mediumship, both in having mediums presenting shows on TV but also a multitude of amateur Ghost Hunting groups sprang up around the country. That really brings to my first meeting with Stephen (The Extreme Ghost Hunter).

He was part of one of these groups and the local paper had done a feature on him and his search for locations to investigate. As a result of reading that article I emailed him. We met up for a chat and a beer and we got along reasonably well. He told me that he and the group he was with had an investigation booked at a local Art Deco cinema that had been closed for a number of years. They were looking for a medium to work with the group and by chance my E mail landed in his In-Box at just the right time. So I was invited along to that investigation which was booked for a few weeks later in the month. The group also had what was almost the obligatory web page and forum so I did get to "know" the other members to some degree on line. Not ideal but as good as it was going to get. Turning up for the night I was a little cautious. It was my first investigation so I was not sure what to expect, meeting a whole new group of people I knew nothing about plus the pressure I put on myself to do a good job.

I met up with Stephen outside the cinema and gradually as the other members turned up I could put names to faces. We also had with us the ex projectionist of the cinema from when it had been open, acting now as a caretaker on behalf of the cinemas owner. Walking into the cinema for the first time, I was a little reluctant to start spouting off all the things I was seeing, hearing and smelling, but the first thing that struck me as odd was seeing a spirit person leaning over the balcony watching us.

Not that odd as a medium maybe but what was odd was that he was an elderly gentleman wearing a full dinner suit, not what I would expect to see in a cinema. Later I was to learn after I did pluck up courage and start telling the group of this that the father of the owner of the cinema used to stand in that spot every night and collect tickets wearing a full dinner suit. This was the just start of the night and there was plenty more to come.

Not all the memorable events of the night however were paranormal. You will be able to read of those events later in another chapter. Some non paranormal events I feel would have become the stuff of how local urban myths start.

For example, as I opened a small door located to the side of the main doors to collect a takeaway, I saw two slightly tipsy young girls heading home after a night out. As far as they were concerned they were passing a long closed and derelict cinema. The resulting screams and the sight of them disappearing into the night while trying to run in tight skirts and heels while a little drunk but a lot terrified will stay with me for life. Pretty sure that tale of a ghost opening the door on them and saying "hi girls" will have been told over and over the next day to their sceptical friends. That event and other experiences of the night as well as some of the scares I have had at investigations you will read of in other chapters. As it turned out Stephen and I became good friends and we found that our individual skills both on investigations and in life complemented each others.

Added to which we had similar thoughts on how ghost hunting should be done, not as an excuse to carry every gadget possible for one, and also avoiding some of the ego trips that always seem to crop up in groups. We keep each other grounded. After a number of years working together on investigations as well as doing our own things, including Stephen forming Extreme Ghost Hunting and myself the brand The Psychic Biker we decided to combine our efforts. This really I where this book project came from as well as the ideas we have for a TV show. With luck and lots of hard work you shall see us on your TV screen when this book appears. But if not we shall still be trying.

HOUSE CLEARANCES

Not all my work as a medium is prowling around dark castles and ancient halls. Quite often, I am asked by members of the public to visit their home or work place as they are experiencing some odd happenings. Now often when chatting to people about my work as a medium they will say the "I think my place is haunted." To be frank I as a rule ignore that comment as I have yet to meet anyone who at times does not think his or her home is haunted, however, 99% of the time it is simple to find logical reasons for events. There are times however, that the comments are justified.

I have come across many examples of problems at homes and work places during my mediumship career so far but a few stands out from the rest, either due to the peculiarity of the activity or the reasons behind it. The first example starts with a tale of me being tracked down that is almost as interesting as the story of the haunting. Briefly, I used to get collected on a regular basis by the same taxi driver after attending bike club meetings. On the journey to my home, we would chat about this and that. Over the months, she learned about my "sideline" as a psychic medium and, the conversation would often turn to that, nothing remarkable about that until much later in my life. By this time I had moved into my present home and had not encountered this woman since moving. She had changed cab companies and I for various reasons ceased to go to the pub as regularly as I had used to.

Therefore, it is with great surprise one morning to answer a ring on my doorbell to find her there, with her taxi looking for me. Very confusing! At first I assumed she was simply at the wrong address but then she began asking if I "still did the spooky stuff". Confirming I did still do" spooky stuff" she asked if I could help a friend. She it appeared had somehow tracked me down through a series of links, friends of friends etc even though I had been moved 2 years. Once I was over the surprise, I listened to her tale.

A friend of hers was so afraid of the activity in her home she was leaving home as soon as her children were dispatched to school and wandering the local park or town centre until she had to return home for the children coming home. After a few more questions, I agreed to visit the house but first I called a fellow medium to sort out a time and date we could both go. In cases such as this, it is normal for mediums to work in pairs. Simply as an insurance in case either one is badly effected by any energies encountered.

This did not take long to arrange and we met outside the address given, it was a typical end terrace house with a nice view over a local park. Upon ringing the bell, we were greeted by a tallish woman with very short hair. Without having to use any psychic sense, you could see the worry etched on her face. The medium accompanying me, a woman called Helen, works differently from me. If you have already read the chapter about my journey to this point you will have read my comments of how mediums work in ways that reflect their personality, in this case it was demonstrated amply.

Helen always stops on the doorsteps of a home and asks any energy within permission to enter, while I, with my typical "in your face style" charge in with attitude written all over me. Once inside we found a group consisting of the woman who had greeted us, her partner from a civil partnership and our mutual friend the taxi driver. As always, I asked that they told us nothing except any areas in the home they do not wish us to go.

I always ask this, as I never forget that we are in someone's home. In this case, we were given a free reign to go where we wanted. Helen and I at the same time when asked, "Where are you going to start" pointed upstairs. As we started to climb the stairs we encountered an elderly spirit man who attempted to block our path, as I was leading the way that did not work and I insisted he move aside. I have no idea why he

19

wanted to block us other then maybe he already felt that some "strange people" had already invaded his home and we were just another example. At the top of the stairs on the landing was a bookcase, which we later learned that this man used to move the books around on. This was just one of the ways he was using attempting to make his presence known to the rest of the household. Helen and I also discovered that this chap used to like to hover on a step leading into the toilet; he felt he could see most of the coming and going from there. However, apart from this man there were no other spirit energies around. I felt sure we had found the source of the problems. Nerveless, we still needed to complete our tour of the house to be sure. So Helen and I descended back down to the ground level, this time with Helen taking the lead. She was drawn into a small room at the bottom of the stairs that appeared to be used now as a room to cope with the usual "overspill" of any family. While she went into that room, I popped my head into the front family room, nothing really of interest from a mediumship point of view there so after a few minutes I returned to the hallway; to find Helen a step inside the small room rooted to the spot and appearing to have some problems breathing. Her breath was coming in short rasping gasps so I wasted no time and simply grabbed her by the collar and dragged her out. Sometimes the solution to a paranormal problem does not have to be mystical. She told that the stench of pipe tobacco and the feeling of being short of breath had been overwhelming.

Once she had recovered we as a pair ventured back into the room. There the old chap we met on the stairs started to talk to us. He was called Charles, Not Charlie or Chas but Charles, he was very insistent of that. He told us that he and his wife while they were both alive had moved to Blyth as he was taking up a job at "the docks," I could not quite gather if this meant Blyth port or the shipyard that used to be there.

He was employed as some sort of draughtsman and with this special skill/talent, was the reason for his employment. He was not from the Northeast and had moved into the area to take up this job that to use a modern term he had been head hunted for. He was most definitely an in charge style of man and yet very reserved. He did not mix well and he seemed to have a low opinion of the people he worked with in Blyth. Therefore, his life while alive revolved around him, his wife and the house we were standing in.

All was well until to his absolute disgust, his wife "died on him." Even as he communicated with us, you could clearly sense the utter bewilderment and loss he felt at the death of his wife. He felt totally abandoned and really did not have the skills to care for himself. As he aged he ended up living, sleeping, eating and existing in the room we were in, the same room Helen had experienced the breathing problems.

As we started to understand and have empathy with this man, he began to ask questions of us. That led us to begin to understand the reason for the recent paranormal activity that had so terrified the present homeowner. He started to ask of me, he preferred to talk to me for no other reason than I was male, for some explanations of the situation inside what used to be his home. As he had already mentioned he told of his wife dying before him in the house and he continuing to live there for quite some time until his death. He had for many years still popped back to the house that was his home for many years. Until now, he had not attempted to make his presence known, being happy just to draw comfort from revisiting his home. It seems that what prompted him now to try and get attention was his complete and utter lack of comprehension on the situation.

In short, when the two life partners "married" and moved in together, it seemed he felt he had to make himself known. He was unhappy, did not understand the situation nor did he approve. Once again, even from beyond the grave often we find that people's personalities do not change. As it happens once we began to chat, he turned out to be a nice enough guy, just as I have said bewildered. Once I explained the situation and made it clear, how upsetting his activities were to the

21

occupants his attitude changed. He had never intended to scare anyone, he simply wanted some answers. In addition, I pointed out that if any of the children living in the property came across any of his activities it would be scary for them. He was most apologetic and concerned, we reached an agreement that he would still pop back in and see this old home but the visits would be not made 'public' so to speak. After a little more chat and even him asking for assurances that I was not playing a practical joke on him re two women being married, he left the room and house. Helen and I spent a little more time to check there were no other spirit people in the home then we did a standard cleansing of the whole house and added some layers of protection to it. We joined the rest of the people in the kitchen and over a coffee; we learned some more of the experiences and events that had caused so much concern.

The owner told of finding the same kitchen chair over turned every time she left the room. No matter if it was for 2 minutes or overnight, yet never hearing the chair fall. It looked as if someone had taken the time to place it in that position rather then it falling or being pushed over. She showed us scrawls using crayons that had appeared overnight on sheets of paper left in a locked room. They started to leave these sheets out because the walls and tabletops were being scratched or drawn on. Most of the attempted were just lines or meaningless scratching but some appeared to be crude attempts at forming letter and words. After some more advice Helen and I left the house and to date there has been no further problems with the ex owner who I feel sure even now is not totally convinced that the whole thing is not the Geordies winding up an outsider.

The second occasion that stands out came about because of a friend of Stephens, my co-author in this book. A family had asked me to visit them because as is often the case they had a problem with odd things happening in their home. Once again accompanied by Helen I set off to visit and see if there was anything, we could do. After a fruitless time waiting around and knocking on a door I called the lady in question and she told us we were at the wrong house, right estate but wrong place, never trust Sat Nav people. Eventually we found the right house and were greeted by the lady, who had been joined by a friend. Once again, the routine was the same as the previous clearance "do not tell us anything and is there anywhere we cannot go."

Again we were given free reign and I noticed that the two dogs she owned did not want to come anywhere near Helen or myself. I simply put that down to them sensing I was not a lover of dog hair or salvia on my clothes and thought no more of it. This time Helen and I split up, she headed upstairs and I felt a pull into the kitchen. In the kitchen, I came across a spirit child, a girl who was quite young. She was very mischievous and fully aware that I could see her but she would not talk to me. Instead, she appeared to be having a great time running out the kitchen then up and down the stairs.

That stopped as I saw Helen descending the stairs with a spirit man behind her who did not look happy. This seemed to scare the young girl and she hid in the kitchen. Chatting to Helen while the man stood by, he was looking a little less aggressive now I had given him a warning glance, Helen told of what she had found. The man was not a nice character, seemingly very hostile towards Helen and to women in general. It was him it appeared that had been causing much of the problems in the house and he that the dogs were afraid of. While we were standing chatting, they were standing back and cowering with the occasional snarl. After a brief chat with Helen, I attempted to communicate with the spirit man. He was very defensive and wary, really came across as someone with something to hide and did not appear to be able to give any sensible answers. The only thing we could get out of him was he claimed to have some connection to the male of the household from a previous company they both worked at. Other than that he had no connection with the house, the land it stood on or anything else from the family. Therefore, I made it clear that he was not wanted around and his activities would not be tolerated any longer. He made some feeble attempts to complain but I forced him to give assurances that he would leave the house and never return.

Eventually he agreed and looking rather disgruntled left. As he did, the young spirit girl cautiously emerged from her hiding place in the kitchen and came over to us. Helen began to chat with her and we learned of her tale. She was the daughter of the woman that had greeted us as we had arrived. She gave us her name and would simply say that she "came to see her mummy and play with the children."

Helen gently explained that at times she was scaring people, as they did not understand that she simply wanted to play. The girl at first was rather petulant trying to blame everything on the spirit man that had just left, until at last Helen gently convinced her that she should not make so much of a pest of herself. Once she agreed Helen and I decided before we continued any further we really needed to chat with the homeowner. We sat down with her in the lounge and she told us her story. It was quite simple really; when younger she had an accidental pregnancy while with a former partner. It was decided that she would continue with the pregnancy but sadly, the baby was born but only lived a short time. A heart-breaking story but when we told her the name the young girl had given us she crumpled. Turns out this were the name that had been given to her baby while in the hospital shortly after the birth. The name is not important and I will keep it private as it is personal to the woman concerned but the result was the woman was happy for her daughter to remain in the home.

Although just as we had, she asked if the girl could be a little quieter and better behaved. The young girl was standing next to Helen listening to this conversation and nodded happily. The last thing to come from this tale, at least for now as there was further events at this home but that is for another book, the last thing was the change in the dogs. As we stood chatting, getting, ready to leave they emerged from the kitchen where their beds were, at first cautiously, then with much more enthusiasm. In fact, their owner stood and watched open mouthed as one of the dogs climbed onto Helens shoulders and snuggled down happily. Neither Helen nor the dog looked uncomfortable. Even to my eyes they were changed animals, seemingly much happier and wagging their tails.

A few weeks later I returned to the home to do a psychic night for the woman and her friends, she again told me she could not believe the change in the dogs, they were eating better, playful, energetic and much friendlier. Not the reason we went to the home but a side benefit to the whole episode.

Lastly this is a brief tale that demonstrates the power of suggestion.

Once again the whole thing starts with a call from a friend asking me to help a friend of theirs. In this case, it was the owner of a local paper shop. For 3 years, she had quite happily opened the shop at an early hour every morning to start the day's trading all alone and with never any problems. Then a customer told her that the shop was haunted. From then on she was convinced that certain areas of the shop had problems. I popped over to see the shop, did a through walk around, and found nothing. Just goes to show that we humans can convince ourselves of almost anything. That is why I shall always stay as the "sceptical medium."

EXTREME GHOST HUNTER

STEPHEN LAMBERT

I was born in Ashington, Northumberland, England on 1st November 1973. I had a normal upbringing in the North East of England. Looking back I have tried to establish when exactly I became interested in the paranormal and have come to the conclusion this was an ongoing interest from a very early age. My first real dealing with death was the loss of my grandfather from my father's side of the family. I was very young at the time and remember waking up during the night and seeing what can only be described as various heads of gentlemen around my sofa bed. I am not saying that these were ghosts. Maybe I didn't wake up and was dreaming or possibly it was the imagination of a young boy. It was very strange never the less.

What is not in doubt is the root cause, albeit a good one, of my interest in all things horror and spooky. It was my father who helped start me on the journey I am now on. He absolutely loved horror movies. Rightly or wrongly, as a young boy, I had watched many such movies as The Evil Dead, Dawn of the Dead, The Exorcist and many more. My parents still have a box set of 70's LP's that has a Ouija board drawn on the inside of the cardboard box that held the LP's. Now I have never seen them use it and I am not sure having the letters in alphabetical order is correct but at least they tried.

Moving forward a few years there was the loss of my other grandfather. This affected me greatly. I was very close to him and to see an intelligent man, who had survived his ship being sunk in the Second World War, just wilt away to nothing was very hard to take. His mind and body had gone and I remember being told to visit him as he didn't have long left. I didn't like the service home he was in. Not that there was anything wrong with the staff or people I just didn't like it. The staff had dressed and sat him up in a chair for our visit. When I saw him there was nothing there, it was just like the lights were on but no one was home. My parents were talking to him but there had been no response of any kind for weeks. I just held his hand. As my parents were chatting to him they told him Stephen was here. At the same time and from absolutely nowhere he shouted my name. He didn't move or stop staring at the wall, just shouted my name. We left and a few days later he was gone. I have not really talked about this until now but that day affected me quite badly. I still find it quite hard and often visit his grave when I am down or needing help.

The next major influence, as was with probably a lot of people, was the introduction of TV shows surrounding ghost hunting. I was hooked. I set off on the internet to see where I could get involved. I stumbled across a website for NEPUK (North East Paranormal UK) which are sadly no longer running. I approached them and quickly became involved with the group. I can still remember the very first investigation we went on. It was at the Newcastle Keep, England. You have to keep in your mind here as I tell you about the build up that this was when ghost hunting had first kicked off in a big way.

I remember meeting the rest of the guys from NEPUK in a pub opposite the Keep. I was aware that this investigation was to be a joint night with other groups. We were just starting out and had the minimal amount of equipment. As 9pm approached we moved outside the pub to the front of the Keep. I was astonished by one of the other groups. They had personalised everything. Hats, T shirts, hoodies, bags and even the camera cases had on their group name, personal name or position within the group. It was crazy and beyond belief. Obviously this made us feel out of place. Then to make us feel even better, once inside, there was all manner of electrical ghost hunting equipment being pulled from the personalised bags.

Before things got started (which was about 2 hours whilst equipment was set up) we were told where we would be

27

going, what time we would be going here and there, what we could and couldn't do along with many other stipulations. I was sure I had paid my money so that I could go ghost hunting and not to be told I was to be watching a hazy TV monitor for an hour. I bit my lip though and for the good of the group went with the flow. This first night for me was probably the beginning of the end for that type of investigation. Before people get mad at this point I am not saying an investigation of this type is bad, it was and still is, just not for me. There is a place for all groups and individuals have a choice to carry out investigations the way they want to. After this night I cannot remember ever doing a joint night with other groups as part of NEPUK. Some of the nights as part of NEPUK are included within this book. These were great times and I made a lot of friends including my business partner and co author for this book Paul Green, The Psychic Biker.

Moving on again there have been a few instances with my son which I cannot explain. When he was a toddler and slept in his cot his toys were always at one end of the cot. You never think about this and why should you it's nothing strange. It only became strange when I was doing an investigation at Kielder Castle. You will read more about this in the Kielder Castle account but I have some history you could say with the ghost of Emma at Kielder. Whilst at Kielder a medium told me the ghost of Emma had visited me at home and had seen my son. She didn't know I had a son and also asked me if his toys were at one end of his cot. My jaw dropped at this point. She explained that he may have seen her and was trying to give her his toys to play with.

The next strange occurrence involves both my son and father. I was at work and got a call from my mother to say that my father had seen Evan, my son, in the bedroom at night with another boy that he did not recognize. This was not the first time my father had seen ghostly figures so I just talked it away. That was until my wife at the time called me to tell me about Evans

28

dream. Evan told his mother that during the night he had floated to see his granddad in his bedroom. Apparently he was standing in the bedroom looking at him. Now to hear that about an hour after the first bit of information just stops you in your tracks. I cannot explain either event but both are very interesting.

A trip to Prague and an Ouija board session was the scene of the next strange event. I was excited about visiting Prague, as it is apparently one of the most haunted cities in Europe. Our group all wanted to go on a ghost walk around Prague. All apart from me that is. I just don't like them. 99% of the ones I have been on are more history tours than ghost tours. It is also very rare you even get to go inside anywhere, apart from the pub at the end that is on commission. The tour fit the bill exactly as I described, albeit the pint of lager in the pub at the end was very nice.

At the end of the night we returned to our accommodation where I quietly asked if anyone would like to try an Ouija Board. I hastily cut out some paper and wrote yes and no on them, found a good glass to use and sat down only to see all the brave ones had disappeared to bed. This left four of us to give it a try. I had been part of countless Ouija Board sessions but for the other three this was their first attempt.

Just before I was about to ask out it occurred to me that we were in the Czech Republic. It sounds stupid but this was my first session in a foreign country. What if the spirits were Czech? I had not thought about that but decided to carry on anyway. To get straight to the point my grandfather came through on the Ouija Board. This was not the first time this had happened so apart from it happening in a foreign country I was not shocked. To explain the conversations using the questions and answers with yes and no is very hard to write down so I will simplify things the best I can. My grandfather loved horse racing and it got to the point where I was asking him about this. Against all my teachings to people I asked him if he had any tips.

Surprisingly he did but was not prepared to give me the exact name of the horse. I can only suggest that this was because he was a great studier of form and was not going to make it easy for me. Through questioning he told me the horse would be running on Tues 11th Jan 2005 and that I would have to pick the horse from the names. I have included the year to allow you to gauge a timescale.

I returned to England on the Sunday and was back at work on the Monday. My colleague at work loves gambling, especially on the horses, he is though, a total sceptic when it comes to the paranormal. I explained about the weekend and we agreed there would be no harm in searching the race cards for any possible horses. We looked and only one horse stood out from the rest, Sailor A'Hoy. It was bred out of Handsome Sailor and Eye Sight. Looking further into its breeding there were lines to Found at Sea. Firstly my grandfather had been a sailor and my grandma always called him a handsome sailor. Due to diabetes he had problems with his eyesight in the form of cataracts. When his ship was sunk during World War Two he was found at sea. Put all that together and the fact it was running on the given day it had to be the right horse. There was one problem though, it was 33-1. We waited until the following day which was Tuesday 11th January to place our bet and listened to the race on the radio. Sailor A'Hoy was absolutely nowhere until the penultimate fence. It then took lead and went on to win at 33-1. We were both extremely shocked, especially my colleague who since then has not been so quick to scoff the paranormal work I do. People will be reading this thinking that it cannot possibly be true. All the records are there if you search online. Some may say it is just luck and that may be the case but the horse has only won two out of forty six races. To pick that horse, on the given day, to win one of its two races out of forty six we must have been extremely lucky.

For the reasons talked about earlier and the dwindling away of members of NEPUK I decided to go it alone. I had an idea for a book (which you are reading now), albeit it has taken about 5 years and many format changes to get to this point. I wanted to have a go at things my way. I had made up my mind to contact locations in Northern England & Scotland about the possibility of spending time at their haunted location. I would document the history, ghost stories and record accounts from the overnight vigil. The big difference being, this was to be done by myself or at most there would be only two of us on location.

To my surprise I was getting a lot of positive responses from locations. Previously whilst trying to acquire locations for groups I had found it much more difficult. I can only surmise that people preferred less people on their property. My work for the book at this time was very enjoyable. I got the chance to stay in some wonderful places, some which were family homes not open to the public. One of my accounts was published in a book by Jason Karl, 21ˢᵗ Century Ghosts. I had met Jason previously on a ghost hunting night to help raise money for charity.

Working on the book gave me the idea for a TV show. Being on location alone really captures what I believe ghost hunting is about and this is what I wanted to give the public the chance to see. No fancy equipment (obviously there would be the need to carry a video camera or how could it be a TV show), at one with the elements and the fear of being alone. As with the book, this idea for TV has evolved over time. Hopefully as well as just reading about us you will be able to see us on the TV in the not too distant future. To help us with the book, TV and many other ideas I created the company Extreme Ghost Hunting Limited. The first question I get off a lot of people is why is it Extreme? The fact that people ask that question means that the name works. People are interested and intrigued. When creating the company I tried to think of lots of different catchy names until I got to Extreme. This was the nearest word I could get to explain the points I mentioned with the TV idea, points such as alone, scary location, no fancy equipment and against the elements. Throw a Psychic Biker into the mix and I think

Extreme Ghost Hunting works very well. As we are finding out everything to do with TV is a very slow process. I believe there is an element of luck involved with it as well. Being in the right place at the right time comes to mind. Who knows, by the time you have started reading this book you may have already seen us on TV. All that is left to say is that I hope you enjoy the rest of the book.

BORTHWICK CASTLE

Sir William de Borthwick built Borthwick Castle in 1430. A Royal Charter was required to build it and was granted by King James I of Scotland. The Chancellor of the Exchequer would however pay for its construction. The reason behind this was that William had been a hostage in the release of King James I in 1424.William's father and grandfather had both been ambassadors to the English Court and one of his ancestors was one of the knights that carried Robert the Bruce's heart to Jerusalem. The site of Borthwick Castle had previously been a mote-hill called the Mote of Lochorwart. The land slopes down steeply on three sides. It is only to the west that the land was vulnerable. So to offer extra protection here he built two square towers out from the main part of the Castle. For even more protection the walls went from 14 feet thick in the dungeon to 9 feet thick in the garrison. The Castle also had a strong vaulted ceiling some 30 feet high.

Within the Great Hall the walls were hung with tapestries and the ceiling painted with frescoes. There is a State Room above the Great Hall that was originally divided into a sitting room and a chapel. The Chapel is still used today. Above the State Room was the first floor of bedrooms and then in the vault space the Garrison. The Castle was built deliberately high so that in the event of an invasion they could signal to Crichton Castle. Mary Queen of Scots stayed at the Castle in June 1567. This was one month after her marriage to the Earl of Bothwell. Lord Darnley had been murdered in February that year. The sixth Baron invited them to escape the scandal surrounding Darnley's murder. They had not been at the castle long before word arrived that Lord Morton and Lord Lennox accompanied with a thousand men were approaching to take Bothwell by force.

On hearing the news Bothwell left for Dunbar leaving Mary to face Morton and Lennox. She told the army he had left then escaped herself disguised as a page. She rode off from Borthwick Church to rejoin Bothwell. She was followed and finally gave herself up at Carberry. She was taken from here to Edinburgh then to Loch Leven Castle. She was beheaded after being held prisoner for twenty years.

John the ninth Baron of Borthwick was a Royalist and had sent troops to fight Oliver Cromwell. In 1650 Cromwell fired two or three cannon shots high up on the east wall of Borthwick Castle. The cannon shots inflicted some damage and a letter was sent to the Baron saying that if he did not leave Borthwick Castle then Cromwell would 'bend his cannon' again. The Baron held out a little longer until more damage was inflicted. Realising he could not win, he left asking for 15 days grace to collect his belongings. Cromwell took over the Castle and left it empty. The Castle was then passed to the family of the Dalrymples and then to the family of Mitchelson of Middleton. It was then empty for nearly 150 years until John Borthwick of Crookson bought it in 1812.

During the Second World War the Castle was used to store some of Scotland's most irreplaceable documents, manuscripts and art treasures. The present Lord Borthwick leased the Castle to Helen Bailey in 1973 and it opened as a Conference Centre/Hotel in 1975.

There are various ghost stories surrounding Borthwick Castle. The main story is of a local girl called Ann Grant that was apparently made pregnant by one of the Borthwick Lords. Heavy with child she was slashed across the abdomen and left to die in what is now the haunted room. A modern visitor and prior owner have reported that they had seen a vision of the murder.

Guests in the haunted room, the Red Room, experienced several manifestations. There are reports of temperature fluctuations and scratching on the inside of the door. Footsteps can often be heard on the turnpike of the stairs at around 1.30 am. A heavy fire door opened by itself. Weeping and wailing could be heard during a conference in a part of the Castle where nobody was known to be. Previous owners had apparently had the haunted room exorcised but it had no effect.

I could not wait to stay the night at Borthwick Castle. There were a few factors that were going to add lots of spice to the night. Firstly I was to be staying somewhere that Mary Queen of Scots had spent some time and even had her own room. I still had a fear of her since my visit to Castle Cary. Secondly I was staying in the Red Room. Known as the haunted room it was supposedly the most haunted room in the whole Castle, so haunted that a previous owner apparently had it exorcised. Lastly something I forgot to mention earlier. I was to be staying at Borthwick Castle on Halloween.

It was late in the day when I arrived at Borthwick Castle. Approaching in the dark it was quite hard to make out the whole size of the place. I entered up some stairs into the Great Hall. At the opposite end there was a fire burning in a huge fireplace. I signed in and was given the key to the Red Room. I was informed there was to be a tour of the whole Castle later on in the night. Excited about the tour I made my way up the spiral stone staircase to my room. When opening the door to the most haunted room in the castle you are not quite sure what to expect on the other side. To be honest the room itself was excellent. Everything you would expect in any good hotel but with and added twist. This room was haunted. The four-poster bed had red covers, drapes and a few walls had red wallpaper. This was quite obviously the Red Room. You had to bend down to get into the bathroom area that was set back around the side of the bed. There was an eerie feeling in the room but I was not sure if this was due to the fact I knew what had occurred and had been seen by previous guests.

Before setting off back down for the tour I set up a few trigger objects in the room. What this involves is placing objects in an area and seeing if they get moved. Basically I placed some coins on a blank bit of paper. I drew around the coins and placed them on one of the cabinets. If they were moved whilst I was on the tour then obviously this would show from the lines I had drawn around the coins.

I locked the door and made my way down to the Great Hall for the tour. I sat reading the Comments Book for Borthwick Castle in front of the fire. I always find the Comments Book a great place to see if other people have experienced anything paranormal on their stay. I suppose it is train spotting for the ghost hunter. The lady who was to be the tour guide was a wealth of knowledge. She told me all the stories plus showed me a picture taken of the Great Hall. It appears to show a small boy running behind guests. It is a very good picture. There was no child staying the night of the picture, which makes it even more interesting. Sat opposite me was a German couple that were the only other guests for the night. The guide had explained that when she finished her shift the door would be locked and I was free to go where I wanted. This was a dream come true.

I set off on the tour with the German couple and we headed up to the State Room. I was asking to go into rooms that were in darkness and I could see the Germans were very puzzled. They were even more shocked when I started taking pictures in the dark. Another story that came to light on the tour was the appearance of blood like spots on the walls the day after the rooms had been cleaned. Whilst in one of the rooms I could see some strange red spots on the wall that I could not explain.

We made our way up the spiral staircase towards Mary Queen of Scots room. This was one of rooms I wasn't too happy about going into first. On entering the room there is a picture on the wall of Mary Queen of Scots. The picture of her took me aback. The only pictures I had seen before were of her when she was older. This was a nice picture of her at a younger age and made me feel slightly less anxious of her. In her room there was a four-poster bed. The en suite area used to be the servants sleeping quarters. There is also a window area with seats either side. This is an area where she apparently put on her makeup. The reason for this was that it was the best place for sunlight into the Castle. I knew later in the night I was going to have to face my fear of Mary Queen of Scots and return to her room.

I returned to the Red Room and checked the trigger objects and they had not moved. After a couple of hours of relaxing and setting up equipment I decided it was time to set off. Lights off and armed with my night vision camera I locked the door of the Red Room behind me. As soon as I turn around I now have a spiral staircase to walk down. This is ok with the light on but when you are on edge and you can't see around the corner it is pretty nerve racking. I manage to conquer my nerves and wander down to the Garrison Room and position myself on the sofa in front of what is left of the fire.

Looking out over the Garrison Room and up to the Balcony I started to ask out if there were any spirits present. Just to help me slowly settle in the fire sparked and I nearly fell off the chair. I spent some time in the Garrison Room with only a few light anomalies on my camera. These could have easily been passed off as dust. With the fire on it was quite hard at times to make out any possible noises that may have been responding to me asking out.

I headed from the Garrison Room up to the State Room. I spent time here asking out for spirits with no response. Whilst sitting in the State Room I knew what was coming next. I had to face my unexplainable fear of Mary Queen of Scots and make my way to her room.

I gingerly opened the door and made my way into her room. Once in I was not sure where to put myself. The room was cold and it seemed like her eyes on the picture were following me around the room. For some strange reason I decided to sit in the window area where Mary Queen of Scots would put on her makeup. I think I did this in the hope there would be some light coming through the window. That was not to be and was now at the furthest point away from the door if I needed to make a sharp exit.

I sat for about ten minutes gathering my thoughts and building some courage up to ask out. It is hard to explain but you just get the feeling that something is going to happen. I then said, "If there are any spirits present can you please try and knock once for yes." From an area close to the picture there was a knock. It wasn't just something clicking it was a knock. To be sure I asked the same question again. In direct response and from the same area there was another knock. Well at this point I wanted to make that sharp exit but had to try and stay put. The hairs on my arms and neck were on end and I could hear my heart thumping.

To prove to myself I was not going mad I was thinking of a question that would have to give two knocks as a response. So I said, "Are you happy with me being here? One knock for yes or two knocks for no." Again from the same area near the picture there were two knocks. I had the feeling that question would give two knocks for an answer. Next I asked, "Is this Mary Queen of Scots? One knock for yes or two knocks for no." Again one knock but this time the knock was more between the picture and me. Now my worst fears were starting to come true. Firstly I have tried this technique nearly everywhere I have stayed over the years and have never once had a response. Secondly and more importantly at this moment in time it appears the spirit in this room could be that of Mary Queen of Scots.

Now I am thinking of another question to try and get two knocks. So I stupidly ask, "Are you happy with an Englishman sitting where you used to put your makeup on? One knock for yes or two knocks for no." The next two knocks were louder but thankfully had moved back towards the picture on the wall. As excellent as these responses were I was now pretty scared. I hoped there would only be one knock in response to the next question. I said, "Would you like me to leave your room?" I didn't even get the chance to ask the second part. There was one single knock from the area of the picture. That was enough and I was off out the door. I was happy to go back and spend the night in my own room, even if it was supposed to be the most haunted one in the Castle. The rest of the night passed without incident. In all my years of ghost hunting this single experience has to rate as one of the all time best and scariest I have ever had.

In the morning before leaving I had a look at the damage inflicted by Cromwell on the east side of the Castle. Just as well John the ninth Baron decided to leave when he did. Borthwick Castle may not have been here today if Cromwell had the chance to 'bend his cannon' again.

EXTREME GHOST HUNTING

Well if you have read this far you will have some idea of the background of Paul and Stephen. But who or what is Extreme Ghost Hunting? Again you should have read some of the thoughts from Paul and Stephen on the, shall we say philosophy of ghost hunting.

They both have watched on such internet sites as You Tube and also seen at events they attended where the "dressing up" and the gadgets appeared to be the main attraction of the night. There is nothing wrong with that if that is what you are into. Often the social side of these events are, for some people, the reason for attending. But it was not the way either Paul or Stephen wanted to work. They both, while working independently of each other, had come to feel that the barrier of so many gadgets diluted the essence and the purpose of what they wanted to do.

Unless you are a purely scientific group, and there are plenty of them of varying degrees of competence, then most people want to experience "something." That something will always vary from person to person but what both found in many conversations and debates is that any experience to be of value to anyone has to be personal. In that they have to see, hear, smell or feel that "experience." Using their own senses and not via a camera feeding into a TV screen, nor via playback on a video camera. Though those and other bits of equipment have value when it comes to capturing possible paranormal activity both Paul and Stephen felt they at times got in the way. They both wanted people to feel, see and hear first hand any activity that was occurring around them. After all there is very little in the way of electronic equipment on the market today that can record, analyse, store and react better then the bog standard "human."

Now they both fully accept that the human does come with software faults, it can misinterpret sights, sounds, smells or any other input it is receiving. It can have its programme disrupted by software crashes when emotions are thrown into the mix. But also it can learn, it can use past experiences and apply logic each time it encounters new "events." Plus it has the ability to use machines its fellow humans have invented to back up by recording the same events that the human is experiencing. Ok, that is all a little tongue in cheek but we, you, fellow humans reading this are pretty marvellous bits of kit. So why put something in between that experience and us? To both Stephen and Paul that just seemed illogical.

So over many discussions, meetings and of course going on ghost hunts both started to formulate their approach to the whole ghost hunting style of events. From that Extreme Ghost Hunting was born and then further developed to become an organisation committed to letting people coming on a ghost hunt to have as much freedom as possible to do their own thing. Always with the provisos that safety and respect for the location and any spirits encountered uppermost. They also felt that the usual method of simply booking a location almost ad hoc was not the way to go. In their opinions the development of a relationship with the owners or managers of locations was vital. Not so they could visit the same place time after time, as some groups do, but to enable parties, Extreme Ghost Hunting and the location owners, to get the most possible out of the partnership. From the outset they encountered a very favourable response from locations at what was described by them "as a breath of fresh air." They found that while locations whose bread and butter was to encourage paranormal investigations groups booking the site they also welcomed a company that wanted to work with them to develop the location. They also learned that both Paul and Stephen did not simply pay lip service to the ethos of respecting a location. This was both as a location and as property owned by someone. From that initial approach Paul and Stephen have found that they have now built

41

up and are continuing to build up a good working relationship with many site owners. They have also found that as the relationship has grown, they and the guests on their ghost hunts have benefited. They have been given access to parts of locations that in the past have been denied to other groups and companies. They have been offered the opportunity to investigate locations that have never been investigated before. Usually with the proviso that the location is not revealed as the owners have no wish to turn it into a haunted location. As anyone who has anything other than a passing interest in this topic will know such "virgin" sites as the Mecca for ghost hunting groups and individuals. It was also found that guests on their events once they realised that they were being allowed to do just what Paul and Stephen said they would, started to extend an element of trust to both Paul and Stephen. To the extent that now they will happily book to come out on a cold Saturday night to an event they did not know the location of until the evening before. Such measures are needed to ensure that a site would not be overrun with those groups who seem not to care whose property they trespass on as long as they are the first to investigate a site.

Not all the locations of course are first times investigations that require such a covert approach to the night; many are well known on the paranormal investigation circuit. That said both Stephen and Paul see no reason to change their philosophy, simply due to being on well known locations grounds. They first will always work within any boundaries, parameters or limitations set by the owner. They will always ensure that the location is left as if they had never been there, ensuring that they take any rubbish with them unless given permission to use the locations. They will always ensure that smoking rules of the site are adhered to and due respect is made in the advent of there being any near neighbours. Ensuring that noise in such locations is kept to a minimum. Both during the event and also as guests depart.

Lastly they will also always do their utmost to ensure that guests on their events get to have as much as possible a personal experience. Plus that they will endeavour to ensure guests get to "do their own thing." As one guest who had attended many investigations and ghost hunts over the years when asked by Stephen "What do you want to do?" He replied, "I have never been asked that before."

To see the enthusiasm from such a guest who now could put into practice some theories and ideas she had wanted to try on ghost hunts but had not been able to due to the regimented approach of some groups is proof to Paul and Stephen that they " got it right".

THE WALLAW CINEMA

THE HISTORY

The Wallaw Cinema was built by Percy Lindsay Browne, Son & Harding and opened on the 16th November 1937. The architect is believed to be Charles Alfred Harding. Further research has indicated that this firm and its forebears were a leading and prolific cinema practice in the north east of England and this is understood to be their best surviving work. . The plasterwork was by Webster Davison and Co Ltd. of Sunderland and the streamlined modern light fixtures are by Devereux Moody and Co Ltd of Newcastle.

There were once four cinemas in Blyth, but with the closure of the Wallaw in 2004 there are now none. The others, The Central, The Essoldo and The Roxy, were all closed down in the 1960s and 1970s. When the cinema first built it had a 1600 seating capacity.

In 1987 it was subdivided into Mini, Minor and Major screens. Both the Mini and Minor screens where set beneath the balcony of the Major screen area. In 1998 the Wallaw was refurbished and designated a Grade II listed building by English Heritage. Finally and sadly the cinema closed in 2004 with a final showing of Mel Gibson's 'The Passion of the Christ', and has remained empty since that time. Of late the building has needed further work simply to attempt to stop any further damage. The roof in particular has needed quite a bit of work and much of the interior is approaching a stage where it will be beyond salvage.

There have been various ideas and plans submitted to the local county council, including one by the owners to convert the building into apartments. Of late the building has been put onto the market with offers to buy or rent. Planning restrictions on this listed building have also been eased a little. Now it would simply be a case of keeping the art deco stairs and balcony foyer with other alterations open to negotiation. The last both Paul and Stephen heard after making enquiries themselves with a view to leasing the building was that a "major brewery has made a serious offer."

Let's hope that something or someone comes along soon to ensure at least some parts of this building are kept for future generations.

THE WALKAROUND

When they were growing up in Blyth, Northumberland both Paul and Stephen could recall visiting this local cinema with their respective parents, and later as they grew older with friends. Compared to the modern generation of cinemas it was pretty tame but at the time, to a pair of small boys, it seemed like a massive place with loads of character. They both recall queuing for ages outside to see the blockbuster film Ghostbusters which they both confess seems weird as they are now writing about spending the night there as so called 'ghost busters.' Paul also commented that he saw The Exorcist there and is not keen to experience events shown in that movie on any investigation.

Stephen had always thought the Wallaw would be a great place to investigate. Not only was it a cinema of great character due to its art deco interior but also it always reminded him of a theatre because of the ornate decorations. He always tended to think that a place that must have given people great times and memories would have been filled with so much energy. With so much energy the chance of spirit activity would have been so much greater. Moreover, there was the many staff that had worked there over the years it was open, many of who were reported to be long serving employees so a building that was so much part of their lives would potentially be a great draw to them after their deaths. So attempting to secure a night at the Wallaw Cinema was Stephens's idea and he took on the task of getting access. It was not to prove to be an easy one.

Even though it was up for sale/lease he found it hard to get to the bottom of who actually owned it. Finally, the only option he felt left was to appeal to a local newspaper. They then contacted him asking if he would be willing to take part in a photo shoot outside the cinema to try to drum up some interest.

Once the story and picture was published, two things occurred. One Paul, The Psychic Biker got in touch but also a gentleman from a local haulage company emailed him. He explained that in fact, they owned the cinema and he could arrange for Stephen to have a preliminary visit with a view to sorting out a full nights stay. It is ironic that if Stephen had known Paul at the time, they were to meet a little later because of that picture and article in the paper, Paul could have short-circuited the whole process. His father in law was one of the first employees of the transport company when it was set up in 1926. There were family pictures showing one of the first vehicles used by Ferguson's for its removal business, a pick up style vehicle with solid tyres.

A date was arranged and Stephen contacted Paul who also lived locally to see if he wanted to join him in the first walk around. Paul had no hesitation in leaping at the chance, as not only did he look forward to getting into a new location it was an opportunity to re live his youth. The chance to see if the inside of the building was as he recalled was not to be missed. The following week found both of them eagerly waiting outside the Wallaw for the preliminary visit. To any passing observer they would have looked remarkably like the two excited kids from years ago queuing to get in the pictures. Albeit with a few more wrinkles and a lot less hair in one case. This was their first time and probably the only time any members of the public had been in the cinema for years. On the outside the cinema was boarded up with metal doors covering what used to be windows smashed by vandals. As they entered through a side door both could feel the energy of the place straight away. It felt that a lot of the instant energy was due to their own many memories of the Wallaw that came flooding back to both of them. From

46

chatting to the representative of the owners, it was obvious they were going to get the full tour. Getting to see the   places behind the scenes and there were many. The main entry foyer area where you used to queue for your ticket and food was covered in broken glass from smashed windows. Either side of the ticket booth were two sets of stairs up to the art deco foyer. As with many cinemas of this era the building had been portioned off into smaller, "cinemas /screens". In this case The Major, Minor and Mini screens. The Major screen was entered through doors at the top of the stairs and the other two through doors in the base of the stairs, the stairs being arranged in a horseshoe configuration. The deco was that of a pink that both recalled from visits years earlier when they used to frequent the cinema. Obviously everywhere was covered in dust but both felt this just added to the whole atmosphere of the place. It seemed like after the last person left the cinema the doors were closed and the cinema became like a ghost town. Pardon the pun. On the tour around the cinema both got to see the projection rooms. These rooms still had reels of film and they were astounded to find out that the projectors still worked.

It struck Paul that many children would have been fascinated to see how their parents and grandparents saw movies. No slim line DVD player and disc but huge 5-foot tall heavy metal machines with spools of film mounted on them. The spools themselves measured some 18 inches across.

They were then taking down to the stage area that was in the Major cinema; this area was latterly used to produce shows and pantomimes by the local operatic society. On the walk down to the stage they saw many little rooms leading off the stairs. Some had been used as dressing rooms, others as storerooms and some as both. At a guess it would have depended on the status of the artiste to what size of dressing room they were given. Stephens's first venture treading the boards had an effect on him. He reported, "When I got down onto the stage area of the Major screen and looked out over all the empty seats I was lost for words. I was nervous and there

47

wasn't anyone there. Well unless the spirits were having a good look at me. I have never worked on stage but anyone performing on stage in front of whatever size audience must have similar feelings and emotions. When looking out I was sure I was seeing things moving in the seats and aisles. Maybe a trick on the eyes but very strange if like me you have never stood on stage and looked out into a dark, empty seated auditorium."

Standing on the stage similarly effected Paul though for different reasons. He could feel the energy of this place, the nerves that some of the performers who had trod the boards had felt, both the professionals and amateurs. During this time, pictures where being taken by Stephen, many showed a cluster of orbs around Paul and Stephen and the accompanying staff members excitedly exclaimed at seeing orbs moving across the stage. Paul ever being the sceptical medium kept his own counsel but privately thought that any area such as this, empty for years was going to have clouds of dust flying up, nothing paranormal about that. After a very exciting first visit to the cinema a date was agreed for the overnight vigil. Both Paul and Stephen felt a tingle of anticipation at being able to spend a whole night at this location.

THE INVESTIGATION

In the weeks leading up to the investigation Stephen assembled a group of friends to join Paul and himself on the investigation. As has also been mentioned this was the first investigation he and Paul worked together on. The owner of the building had kindly allowed two men, one of which used to be a projectionist at the cinema to accompany the team on the night. This was the first time Stephen had worked with a psychic medium on an investigation and it seemed he was as excited as Paul to get the night going. Paul met with Stephen outside the building and as they waited for the rest of the team to turn up they chatted about what expectations they had for the night.

It was also a chance for Paul to explain to Stephen how he as a medium worked and how he hoped that would translate into information once they got inside. This being the first time they worked together and the first time Stephen had worked with a medium they were both unsure as to what to expect from each other. The rest of the team arrived and introductions were made and shortly after that the men from Ferguson's arrived to open up. As they entered the foyer and the team were sorting out their equipment Paul was drawn to the balcony area at the top the stairs balcony foyer. He told the team that he could see the spirit person of an elderly man dressed in a full evening suit leaning over the handrail looking down on them, seemingly a little irritated at the noise. Paul did say later that he was at first rather hesitant to say anything about this man as the thought of anyone in an evening suit at a cinema struck him as odd.

However he was reassured when the ex projectionist confirmed that the father of the previous owner has often stood in that place collecting tickets. Back then tickets were issued then collected by an usherette, or in this case, this man, torn in half with one half being returned to the customer and the other collected on a spike. The night was off to a good start already and spirit activity was already showing itself. After completing their basic equipment checks and preparation the teams split into smaller groups and set off to different parts of the building. They were lucky, as the two chaps from Ferguson had managed to get some parts of the electricity system working, so not all the building was in darkness, which made moving around a lot easier. Paul and Stephen set off upstairs into the behind the scenes areas and café area for the Major screen. Even this simple task was an adventure as a long spiral staircase that just oozed character accessed it. The rest of the group headed to the stage area of the Major screen. As they walked, Stephen was explaining to Paul he felt he had some psychic, medium ability. They then entered a small dark room, Paul asked Stephen to walk around the room and stop in any area that he felt drawn to. It appeared to Stephen that he was being asked to stop where he thought a ghost might be. Stephen was not totally at ease with doing this. But he agreed and for some strange reason found himself in a doorway to another room. Stephen commented, "The atmosphere in this area was different to the rest of the room. I can't explain really how I felt apart from being a bit light headed." That feeling is a common one experienced by those that while not trained mediums have a degree of sensitivity. The theory is that being close to the spirit energy of a "ghost" causes it.

Paul told Stephen there was a girl standing in the same spot, which did not scare him as much he thought it would. Paul told Stephen that he sensed this girl had a liking for Stephen but he was not too happy about Stephen staying there too long in case she became attached. At the time, Stephen was not sure what "attached," meant but as he said later "I wasn't taking any chances and moved away from the spot I was standing in."

Later Paul explained that he felt a yearning from the girl to be reconnected with the physical side of life, though despite him asking the girl he could not establish why this was, but he was simply concerned that Stephen as a talented but untrained sensitive could inadvertently invite the energy of the spirit girl to attach to him. Following on from this they both then moved downstairs into the café area of the Mini and Minor screens. In this area, Paul picked up on the psychic energies of a fight that had ended up in a person dying from their injuries. He described the scene as a group of 4/5 young men. Some were dressed in what he could in describe as "teddy boy suits" while the rest were in dark suits with a thin ties. One of them was stabbed by a small bladed knife during a fight between the two groups. While Paul could not be sure if this person had died there as he was only picking up on the history of the event rather than that young man haunting the cinema he was sure it was an event that would have been reported as a serious altercation. There have been attempts to discover if there were any news reports on this but without a firm date it was not possible to find any conclusive information.

Whilst Paul was still in the café area Stephen moved into the Mini screen seating area. He was trying to open up his senses again and was drawn to four seats not too far from the front. He had no clue why but called for Paul and without telling him which seats he had been drawn too asked him to walk around and see if he picked up on anything. Apart from being one seat out Paul was drawn to the same area of seats that Stephen had been drawn to. Paul said he was picking up on a family that had died in a house fire locally. It was not clear to him if they had all died in the fire or if all but the father who had died at a later point from his injuries. What was clear to Paul was that the family were back in visitation at the Wallaw doing something they enjoyed whilst they were all alive.

Paul did say later that the emotions of the scene shown in front of him almost overwhelmed him at first. The feeling of guilt and protection flowing from the father was intense. Paul felt that he was an invader on a family day out and after briefly attempting to find out some more detailed information from the father on the families demise he felt compelled to as he put it "leave the family in peace". It was felt that this would be a good time to take a break and recover from the intense emotions that both Stephen and Paul had felt so the rest of the group were called in for some rest a meal and a debrief.

After supper the whole group descended on the stage area. Some members of the group carried out an Ouija board séance with some success. Numerous unknown characters were coming through but unfortunately; the team could not validate the names. There was also a lot of noise activity during this time, bangs from the back of the stage and at one time, what sounded like footsteps from the same area of the stage which appeared to head towards the centre of the stage and then apparently stopped. Paul had not taken part in the séance preferring to stand back to observe the surrounding areas and the participants at the table. This was something that he had not planned to but he simply instinctively felt that he needed to remove himself from the energy of the circle around the board. He did say that the stage area almost felt like a gathering point for energies though none remained there, instead they seemed to flow on and off the stage. All apart from one, the spirit of an elderly man who had died of a heart attack whilst on stage as an announcer or amateur actor. Paul could not tell for sure as the spirit energy of the man was simply showing an image of himself while alive standing at the front of the stage orating. Though from his attire and manner Paul felt that he was most likely an amateur performer who lived locally and this was a passionate hobby of his.

Nevertheless, many of the team complained of feeling unwell or "woozy". At one time, a member of the team Jon, that Paul had already sensed had psychic talent felt compelled to take a break from the séance. Keeping a close eye on him Paul was not that surprised to see him take only a few steps before collapsing at the side of the stage. Paul was quickly at his side and as he later reported, 'I knew that he had simply drained himself of nervous energy during the séance and I needed to keep him calm and quiet while surrounding him with a protective bubble of energy to give his system time to recover."

Jon was soon on his feet if a little woozy and there were no lasting effects of his collapse. When all this was over Stephen who was on the stage said to a friend "I have got to go to the seats in the back corner. I didn't know why but I just have to go". So compelled was Stephen that he simply climbed off the stage leaving the rest of the team and made his way to that point in the building. To his amazement when he got to that area one of the seats was down in the sitting position. Amazing, because prior to going onto the stage area earlier he had rigorously checked every row of seats to make sure they were all up. He still does not know what pulled him to go to that area. Had the seat came down of its own accord? He will never know.

Investigations into all areas of the Wallaw were coming to a close as morning was approaching. At this point Stephen decided to take a break by himself in the foyer entrance area. As he was just about to sit down, he got a call on the radio from the group on the main stage. They did not say why but asked could he make his way to the upper seating area of Major screen. He slowly and for some reason a bit uneasily made his way through the dark into the upper areas and found himself the cleanest seat he could and sat down. Then the rest of the team told that the girl from earlier in the dark room upstairs, the one that Paul had concerns about, had come through on the Ouija Board. She wanted him to go into the upper seating area that he was sitting in now. When he got there she would try and show herself. Very naughty of them to tell him this once he had got himself sat down. Would anyone no matter how keen a ghost hunter they are be happy to be alone in a area after being told that a ghost was going to pop up? The group on the stage were asking questions of the girl and trying to get her to make noises or move seats near where Stephen was sitting. The next part is best described in Stephens's own words: "The hairs on the back of my neck were up and my senses heightened to there fullest. There were definite noises not far from me in responses to the group's requests for the spirit girl to do something. I had one hand gripping the seat and the other with my finger on the on/off button of the torch. I turned around and saw what I can only describe as a massive white butterfly moving along the aisle in a slow arc up and down. It obviously wasn't a massive butterfly but that is the only way I can describe it. I had never seen anything like this before or have since. I then went to put my torch on and the batteries had run out. I had spares in my pocket. If you have ever seen those films where the bad person is coming and the good person has ran out of bullets and can't get the new ones in for shaking? Well that is what was happening but in my case it was batteries not bullets. I dropped the new ones on the floor and decided to cut my losses and make a hasty retreat for the exit."

All this gave the group downstairs much amusement but of course they had safety in numbers on their side? Little or no activity occurred after this event and as morning drew nearer, the group called it a night at the Wallaw. Stephen and Paul expected some activity at the Wallaw Cinema but this can never be guaranteed. Overall, it was a great night and one Stephen can personally say he got more than he bargained for. Paul also took from the night the sure knowledge that he wanted to do more like it. The faster paced style of mediumship was something he had relished. What was not apparent from the event was that it was the to be the start of a partnership between The Psychic Biker and The Extreme Ghost Hunter, nor that it had been a benign start to their ghost hunting adventures. Other investigation sites would prove to be not as friendly.

BEBSIDE INN

THE HISTORY

Bebside is a village in Northumberland that is situated to the west of Blyth. The Bebside Inn nestles in the heart of Bebside itself. There is a railway line that runs adjacent to the Inn. At one point there was also a station. The Bebside Inn has history spanning back to the 1860's. It was first listed in the Blyth Licence Book in 1873. In 1877 Joshua Rutter constructed a large outdoor cycling track behind the Inn. Rutter had been promoting cycling events for a number of years. The cycle track was known as the Bebside Bicycle and Recreation Grounds.

From 1861 to 1969 there were eighteen different landlords. In 1970 major alterations were made to the Inn. An old passageway that ran straight through the building from the front door to the back was completely removed. In 1982 buyers packed the bar of the Bebside Inn when it came under the auctioneers hammer. In spite of it being packed it only sold for £500 more than the reserve price of £35,000.

Searching for historic evidence of sinister kinds the only record found was that of a suicide next to the Inn. On the 12th January 1878 a girl named Elizabeth Tate drowned herself in a pond near to the railway station. She had some difference with her parents and left for some time. On her return home she was not admitted and then decided to throw herself in the pond. The jury gave a verdict of "Suicide whilst in a state of temporary insanity."

THE INVESTIGATION

Stephen and Paul's experiences and knowledge of the Bebside varied hugely. Stephens's memories of the pub were minimal. When he was younger he tended to socialise in the centre of Blyth and did not venture out towards Bebside. He did always remember the pub as a biker's bar with rock bands a big feature but was not aware of any ghost stories surrounding the Inn. Paul also knew of the pub as a biker bar and when he moved closer to it he started to pop in on the way home from work. He soon discovered it was a thriving bar with a large customer base of local bikers and a strong live music programme, he felt right at home. In fact it was this bar that became the home of the motorcycle club that Paul and two other friends started. Northumberland Bikers, known for their huge Easter Egg Charity event. This consisted of local bikers touring local pubs who volunteered to collect eggs for them. There was a prize for the pub that collected the most eggs that was a wooden egg on a plinth. It became an award that became hotly contested for by the participating pubs. Even to the extent of their locals having crates of eggs delivered to ensure their pub won. All to the benefit of the recipients who were local worthy causes such as children's homes, hospitals and elderly persons homes. As the run itself grew to have over 500 bikes on it and the collection of eggs topped 3000 at times it was a huge and well known event within the county. As well as that charity element there was also a weekend of bands, custom shows etc held at the Bebside Inn over the Easter holidays. The event was attended by bikers from as far north as Inverness, as far south as Cornwell and regular attendees from Wales. So you could say that Paul knew the place quite well, as his wife often would testify to.

So over the years he became, as he says, almost "part of the fixture and fittings." This was long before his activities as a medium but he had heard the various rumours of "ghosts" over the time he drank there. During this time he did have many experiences of a ghostly nature but still having his sceptical head on he ignored or discounted them, despite other people telling of similar experiences.

Regulars told of seeing a dark shape passing them near the toilets and of an elderly man often seen sitting at the same spot at the bar who had disappeared the next time they looked that way. Of course it being a bar so often these tales were put down to having one to many, though one teetotaller also told the same tales as well. However his education into mediumship and ghost hunting coincided with some new owners taking over, Tony and Yvonne. He had spent a few years researching the topic and had been in a development class for quite some time so was starting to find his feet as a medium.

After a few months of tenancy Paul raised the topic of an investigation at the pub. Tony who was a complete sceptic and Yvonne in complete contrast was a believer chatted about the pub and it reputation as being haunted. Yvonne in fact was a devotee of Reiki, a system of healing that Paul had heard of a few times. So they often spent time in conversation passing on knowledge and tales of experiences. There was one memorable time when Yvonne was "cleansing Paul's aura "while he was standing at the bar. The sour unbelieving expressions on some of the more elderly customers, was a sight to behold. The end result of those conversations was an agreement that Paul would do a reading for Tony and Yvonne, Paul did comment later that he thought they simply wanted to suss out his ability before committing to the investigation. A thought later confirmed by Tony

As a result of that reading, which by chance revolved around Tony and his loved ones who had crossed, a date was agreed. As always, such readings shall remain private between Paul and the person being read. It is often a very personal experience so Paul would always leave it down to the sitter to decide if they wished to reveal to the world the details. However Paul did comment that Tony, who was notoriously tight, bought him a drink so he must have done a good job.

Paul contacted Stephen whom he knew from their first investigation together at the Wallaw cinema, also in Blyth and a date was soon arranged .The only down side was that in order to fit in with other commitments it had to be a Saturday night which meant a late start as the team had to wait until the pub closed and was cleared of customers before they could begin.

Part of the team agreed to meet at the venue earlier in the evening as a local reporter wanted to do a short feature on the night as well as take some pictures.

The reporter was a contact of Paul's who was a keen supporter of the local independent lifeboat and its crew. A cause that Paul's bike club had supported via the Easter Egg run over the years. Either via donations or having the crew on the towns high street jangling buckets to coincide with the main part of the bike run coming through. As crowds used to line the road for this spectacle it was a lucrative collection bonus for the crew.

It was odd for Paul to be in his favourite pub on a Saturday night and have to remain sober, a fact that the locals took great delight in teasing him about. The pub every Saturday night hosted live music and it was always packed to the rafters with local bikers and their friends. So when the rest of the team turned up at about 11pm to start preparations for the night it was as always very busy. However Tony and Yvonne met the team in the bar and showed them to the kitchen of the large flat upstairs, which was to be the base for the team. Now to give you the layout of the public part of the Bebside Inn that may be useful for later in this chapter.

There is only one bar that stretches the whole length of the building. There are seating areas facing the bar which include the two windows at the front of the building. To one side there is a pool table, covered on a Saturday night with a board and the on other side is where the live bands perform. Above the bar it is just like any family home with bedrooms, living room, kitchen and bathroom etc with the main bedroom being at the front of the building. Tony and Yvonne had already told some of the team of a few ghostly accounts they had heard of. They included that the men and women's toilets used to be the opposite way around. There were many stories of the girls feeling very strange in the toilets, as if being watched. Some people have suggested this that this may be because of them once being used by men. However as at peak times there would often be an overspill of women demanding to use the men's loo Paul had his doubts on this theory.

Another story was that of a picture of a lady dressed in old clothing. The picture had hung on various walls of the Bebside Inn over the last 15 years. A previous owner, Gordon who was Tony's brother, had removed the picture whilst decorating and it had for quite some time languished in a garage. In its place instead were various pictures of rock stars. Oddly Paul helped to frame and mount the pictures as part of the refurbishment of the bar by Gordon. At some point after Tony took over the pub he found the picture in the garage and Tony's wife Yvonne took a shine to it. She cleaned it up and hung it in one of the bedrooms, however her son who used the room complained about odd things happening. The picture would not stay on the wall; his stereo would turn itself on and off when he was not in the room; his bedside lamp would also do the same. Finally the picture was taken down and stored in an old larder in the kitchen at the rear of the building. The team were not to know but that picture and that woman was to play a large part in the investigation. The investigation began like any other, equipment was set up and tested, and fresh batteries were unpacked and loaded while an action plan for the evening was discussed. Over coffee in the kitchen while waiting Paul commented that he could see a spirit lady sitting in a chair in the corner but the chair she was sitting in differed from the one that was present. The one Paul saw her sitting in was taller with huge winged sides. She seemed unperturbed by all the activity, though for some reasons she became agitated when some people sat in the chair but didn't mind others.

There seemed to be no pattern to her likes and dislikes of differing people but the team respected her wishes and left the chair empty in the end. She did however tell Paul that she was the wife of a past landlord of the Bebside and she would spend her days pottering in the kitchen that at that time was the main room in the pub used by all the family. Before Paul could do any further work on this, Tony and Yvonne joined the group and the night began in earnest.

Almost at once many team members reported problems with power being drained from the batteries in instruments and cameras. Despite fitting batteries from new, sealed packs and replacing batteries with further new ones, again from sealed packs, this was a problem that was to continue sporadically during the whole investigation. As was normal practise the team split into two groups and started to make their way from room to room. Paul was immediately drawn to a room at the front of the building that was sandwiched between two other bedrooms; he and another group member entered the room where Paul encountered a sprit person of a man.

The man told Paul of the time he was in trouble with the police following a fight in a pub in Blyth town centre or as he put it "the polis." The then young man had thought he had seriously hurt or even killed the other combatant in the fight. To escape the police, the family hid him away there until they got him away from the town and out of the county. He spent the rest of his years living in the South of the country before he died at a fairly young age; in his fifties was all Paul could ascertain. The man still returns to the Bebside as a place he felt he was exiled from, even though it appears that it was his choice. Research was done via a local historian to attempt to verify this story but sadly nothing could be found. The historian did comment however, that it was unlikely to have been a huge news item if there had been no trial.

As other members of the team started to make their way around the accommodation area carrying out vigils and experiments there were some slight light anomalies but nothing that couldn't be passed off as dust. There was an attempt to holds a séance in one of the front bedrooms, now used as Tony and Yvonne's bedroom but as soon as they entered Paul knew that the room was regularly "psychically cleansed" by Yvonne and nothing would be encountered there. The team   eventually all ended up in the last of the front bedroom that was used by

Yvonne's son. The bedroom that had seen the problems when the picture was hung there that was mentioned earlier in this chapter. It was decided to hold a séance here. Paul as a rule preferred to stay outside circles to observe and keep an eye on all the participants who decided to join the circle.

Paul supervised the séance and Tony and Yvonne decided to take part, rather surprisingly as Tony the owner, as has been mentioned, was not a great believer. As the séance progressed Paul became aware of a presence in the room and Tony began to complain of feeling strange. Paul began to question Tony to try to establish what he was feeling. Tony simply said that he felt as though "something or someone was wanting him to go somewhere but he did not know where"; later Tony said he felt it was the husband of the women in the picture that had caused problems when it was hung in that room. Paul was a little concerned at this point as he was some distance from Tony and there were a few people in between them. As Tony appeared to be feeling odd and was most defiantly acting out of character Paul would have preferred to be within reach in case of trouble When Paul tried to connect with this energy to get some answers the atmosphere in the room appeared to change. It became oppressive and threatening.

Oddly at this time Tony seemed to recover to more his normal self, it appeared that the energy causing the problems had refocused itself away from Tony and on to Paul and the rest of the team. As is so often encountered in these sorts of scenarios the room appeared to grow darker, as if the light was being sucked out the atmosphere. Other team members also started to ask questions of the energy pressing to try and get some ideas of its identity, however the more questions that were asked the angrier the energy appeared to become. At this point some team members sitting closest to the door reported hearing the sound of footsteps on the landing just before all the power suddenly failed. Several team members had spotted the failure as the lights in the corridor and the display on the clock radios had gone out.

The séance was abandoned and the circle closed down to allow the team to investigate further. Tony found that the power for the whole of the Bebside Inn had gone off, even though at the time the upstairs living part of the building was on a different electric circuit to the down stairs bar area. This obviously gave some members a bit of a shock. After an hour of checking and searching it was found that a fuse had blown in a socket in the kitchen. Incidentally, adjacent to this socket was stored the aforementioned picture of the lady! A fridge was plugged in to this socket and despite various attempts by Tony the power could not be restored.

As it seemed certain that the power was not going to be restored in the near future the team decided to hold a séance in the bar, for some reason the pump lights were still working so it gave sufficient light to carry on. The tables in the bar had very heavy cast iron bases which made them perfect for an attempt at table tipping. Almost from the start the table was very active, from questioning this energy it seemed it was a male spirit person who seemed to be very angry. At the same time several of the team reported feeling uneasy and seeing a dark shape crouched in one corner of the bar.

Despite their best efforts the team struggled to get any sensible replies from the male energy and they reported he seemed "enraged and incapable of rationale thought." The table was rocking from one extreme to the other, at times the legs on one side leaving the floor. At last the energy faded and a much softer female energy came through. The names and information given by her was linked to one of the team members, Stephen and another location, which will be reported in more detail later in this book; that location and chapter, is Kielder Castle and the female energy is a lady called Emma. Of which there is a chapter in this book devoted to her and her relationship with Stephen.

As by now the time was passing and dawn was near it being June the team decided to call it a night and packed away the equipment. The following day the company electrician had to be called out. Then it was noticed that not only had the lights and sockets failed but also the power to the emergency lighting and signs. He was baffled as to why the power could have failed in such a catastrophic manner over what should have been a fairly minor problem, a blown fuse. Once the fridge was unplugged and the reset switch was hit, everything should have returned to normal. This was as reported something that had been tried several times the previous night. Power was eventually restored. The electrician spent several hours going over the whole system but could find no reason for the outage. To this day there has been no explanation for this occurrence.

Paul, a few days later, explained what he had psychically picked up about the lady in the picture using psychometry. She was apparently a previous owner of the Inn but who was also teetotal. She was a lady with a strong character and was not going to be happy unless she was overseeing what was going on at the Inn. She liked to see "the pennies going over the bar". She had not taken well with being removed and stored in a garage, found and placed on a bedroom wall and then to add insult to indignity stuffed down the side of a fridge!

Blowing the fuse seems an extreme way to get her point across but she got her way in the end. The picture has been re hung in the bar and to this day there have been no more problems. Tony later reported to the local paper "I approached the team through Paul to do this as I am interested in this sort of thing anyway but I am quite sceptical. I need proof. I have seen strange shadows while in the pub and on the night the presence of a man was felt by team members in the same place I have seen the shadows". Since the investigation the Bebside closed for a short period before opening with a new owner.

With the new owner Paul independent of the team carried out a further brief investigation and "psychic night." This was not an in depth investigation but something the new owners was wishing to carry out for their own interests. Most of what emerged from the night was of a highly personal nature and not for publication but of interest was that again the feeling of a dark, sinister energy was again reported in the same area of the bar as previously reported. The new owners did not know of the previous reports though. Since then the Bebside Inn has once again closed and has been shut for some time now. An attempt to gain access to carry out another investigation was refused by the owners and letting agents.

Until it finds a new owner The Bebside Inns mysteries and ghostly residents will have to wait to reveal themselves and any further information.

CASTLE KEEP

In about AD120 the Romans built the first bridge to cross the River Tyne at the place where Newcastle now stands. The bridge was called Pons Aelius or 'Bridge of Aelius', Aelius being the family name of Emperor Hadrian, who was responsible for the Roman wall built along Tyne-Solway Gap. The Romans built a fort to protect the river crossing which was at the foot of the Tyne Gorge. The fort was situated on rocky outcrop overlooking the new bridge, on the site of the later Norman castle. Little else is known about the Roman fort that existed there.

At some unknown time in the Anglo-Saxon age, the site of Newcastle came to be known as Monkchester. During this time, a cemetery was established on the site of the Roman castle.

In 1080 the Norman king, William I, sent his eldest son, Robert Curthose, north to defend the kingdom against the Scots. After his campaign, he moved to Monkchester and began the building of a 'New Castle.' This was of the "motte-and-bailey" type of construction, a wooden tower on top of an earthen mound (motte), surrounded by a moat and wooden stockade (bailey). It was this new castle that gave Newcastle its name.

In 1095 the Earl of Northumbria, Robert de Mowbray, rose up against William Rufus and Rufus sent an army north to crush the revolt and to capture the castle. From then on the castle became crown property and was an important base from which the king could control the northern barons.

Not a trace of the tower or mound of the motte and bailey castle remains now. Henry II replaced it with a rectangular stone keep, which was built between 1172 and 1177 at a cost of £1,444. There were at that time no town walls and when attacked by the Scots, the townspeople had to crowd into the bailey for safety. It is probable that the new castle acted as a magnet for local merchants because of the safety it provided in dangerous times.

Additional protection to the castle was provided late in the 13th century when stonewalls were constructed, with towers, to enclose the town. Ironically, the safety provided by the town walls led to the neglect of the fabric of the castle. In 1589, during the reign of Queen Elizabeth the castle was described as being ruinous. From the early 17th century onward this situation was made worse by the construction of shops and houses on much of the site, often using the fabric of the castle for building materials.

In 1643, during the English Civil War, the Royalist Mayor of Newcastle, Sir John Marley, repaired the keep and probably also refortified the castle. In 1644 the Scottish army crossed the border in support of the Parliamentarians and 40,000 Scottish troops besieged Newcastle for three months until the garrison of 1,500 surrendered.

During the 16th to the 18th century, the keep was used as a prison. By 1800 there were more than fifty houses within the boundaries of the castle housing several hundred people.

In 1809 Newcastle Corporation bought the keep and provided it with a roof and battlements. In addition the private dwellings within the castle boundaries were demolished. In the mid 19th century the arrival of the railway in Newcastle led to a viaduct to be constructed to the north of the keep and crossing the site of the castle. As a result, only the keep and the Black Gate now remain. The Black Gate is so called after Patrick Black, a tenant there in the 17th century.

The keep is currently owned by Newcastle City Council and managed by the Society of Antiquaries of Newcastle upon Tyne, one of the world's oldest antiquarian societies.

The Castle Keep and Blackgate can be visited today. The keep is also notable in having the main East Coast railway line running through the centre of the grounds. In particular, the battlements offer fine views over the River Tyne quayside, the cathedral and Newcastle Central station.

THE INVESTIGATION

This was the second location that Paul and Stephen did together. It was as with the Wallaw an investigation done as part of a now defunct group known as NEPUK, or North East Paranormal UK. This investigation was of the type common at the time. The Keep had been hired for the night and spaces sold off to various individuals and groups. So there was going to be a fair mixture from a diverse set of individuals. Paul and Stephen travelled together to Newcastle and were to meet up with the rest of the members from NEPUK at a pub opposite the Keep.

Stephen had packed some equipment, mainly a camera and some sound recorders. At the time he was still playing on the fringes of those people that liked to have the latest gadgets to play with. He was however starting to formulate opinions regarding the excess of equipment that some people carried. Paul as usual simply as he always says "took himself and his mind." Once the others had been met at the pub there was little to do except wait for the caretaker and guide from The Keep to turn up to open the doors at 21.00 hours.

This is a guy called Paul who anyone who knows The Keep will know as he is a long serving and very knowledgeable member of the Keeps team. Though having two Paul's was going to be confusing all night. Once he had unlocked the doors other people from other groups started to arrive and unpack. As they did so Paul's and Stephens eyes met and they could tell they both had the same thoughts. They had their first glimpse at how a certain TV show had taken a grip on ghost hunting groups. One group had personalized everything. From hats, shirts, hooded tops and even personalized bags for their cameras and other equipment. At this point Stephen whispered to Paul that he "wondered if personalized items would help attract more ghosts". The shirts and hooded tops maybe were not to bad but even the bags for the equipment was monogrammed. That was going a bit far. They could see from the outset what were going to be up against. Then it seemed that there was just more and more equipment being pulled from the recess of bags and festooned around people's bodies. The arrays equipment that was being pulled from the bags was unbelievable. These people either have too much time, too much money or basically just loved ghost hunting more than life itself. Groups seemed to be forming by themselves. Everyone with equipment (and personalized gear) just seemed to get his or her stuff together and set off. Competition between groups was becoming evident. Maybe not on a personal level but definitely with the 'look he may have a Porsche but god damn I've got a Ferrari.'

Paul, Stephen and the rest of the NEPUK group figured that it was pretty much a free for all and let the best man/group win, though they both felt that some sort of coordination would have made more sense to avoid groups being on top of each other. So those that had equipment grabbed it and set off to work their way through the rooms in the Keep.

The Keep is a big place and they somehow seemed to end up away from other groups. Normally the case when doing your own investigation is that you have set areas, split up and then meet back to swap and go to other areas; as time passed though it was evident that the 'elite' of ghost hunters could just wander through into areas where other groups were.

Some of NEPUK seemed to feel that there was a pecking order and they were bottom of the pile and dare not say anything. Paul however while still not wanting to upset people in a group he had just met still could not resist a warning growl at some of the more moronic invasions. Being fairly new to the art of investigations something they did not pick up on at first is how different people react when put into a situation like a paranormal investigation. In time and with experience people tend to become more rational but on his first visit to the Keep, Stephen had to laugh. There was a girl there that thought every noise and light was paranormal related. At one point whilst standing next to Stephen she said that her arm had been pulled. He had my doubts and then for the rest of the night she decided to show him numerous pictures of so called orbs caught on her digital camera. You may all be thinking at this point that for a couple of guys that organizes and loves going ghost hunting this all sounds very negative. But you must remember this was all in the early days of the explosion of ghost hunting, which was spawned by a very popular TV show.

As Paul and Stephen investigated more locations and later returned to the Keep their views changed, however at this point they both had their doubts about the way events were organized but lacked the experience to know if their ideas were shared by others. This first visit to the Keep was an eye opener for both of them. Not that there was much paranormal activity but more the fact that they got to see the different levels at which paranormal groups were operating at. This first brush with other groups has helped them a lot and is the part of the driving force behind their ideas and opinions on ghost hunting events now.

Future visits to the Keep but this time as part of an event organized by Paul and Stephen as a single group was more enjoyable and provided them with many strange events. It really is an exceptional place and they would urge any group to take the opportunity to visit if they have the chance. However let's return to the night itself and see what events occurred. There is a multitude of history associated with the castle and there are many areas that are said to have paranormal activity.

The first area that the team decided to head for was the great hall and the gallery that runs around the top of it. In the great hall none of the team could detect anything odd and Paul himself at that time simply felt it was just a large empty space. However the gallery above was a different matter. Stephen and other members of the team did not like this area. It may simply be that it is basically a square that has tunnel like walk ways all the way around. At certain points around there are alcoves that look out down onto the Great Hall. When you are walking around you cannot see around the corners, which for most people would be unnerving. Many felt that it was one of those situations where you think where the hell I can run if something happens.

Paul felt that as he walked the gallery there was a woman wearing a very ornate red dress bustling along in front of him. She was fully aware of Paul and the rest of the team and appeared to be almost playing hide and seek, showing herself to Paul but never allowing him to get closer than about 12 feet away. But with regards to paranormal activity that could be seen or recorded by the rest of the team there was very little. All rather disappointing and it had been said that this area was a very active part of the location. It was decided to move down into the Garrison Room on the ground Floor. In doing so the move highlighted another aspect of the keep. All the steps on all the stairs in the Keep, and there are lots, are cut at varying heights and widths to make the task of any invading army harder.

However what it also does is make life very hard for ghost hunters in the dark to move through the Keep without losing their footing. It is also very easy in the dark in an unfamiliar place to lose your bearings. Something Paul found out to his cost when he later managed to end up on the roof. As this event was taking place in mid June it was a very warm night so stair climbing turned out to be an exhausting task

The team at last settled into the Garrison Room. First let's talk at the layout. It is a medium size square room with one entrance in and out. Stone circular column located in the middle of room. There is a set of stairs that lead to another room above and to the side of the Garrison room itself. Around the room there are various stone artefacts relating to the Keep itself.

Stephen and another NEPUK member named Jon were sitting on the stairs in the garrison room doing the usual thing of calling out asking for any spirits present to make themselves known. Paul at this time had wandered up to the roof of the castle to indulge in a spot of people watching as the pubs emptied. However during a pause of asking out, a pause due to there being no response to the requests, there was the sound very loud crack coming from the window behind Stephen and Jon. Jon reacted wonderfully. Displaying jumping skills that could have only been likened to that of Magic Johnson slam dunking a basketball, he leapt from the point they were sitting on the stairs to the floor and took off running. Stephen attempted in vain to grab him as he disappeared down the stairs but to no avail. Stephen commented "If I had time to shoot a picture and showed it to people they would have thought that Jon was part on the Enfield Poltergeist, he seemed to hover in mid air for a long time."

During all this commotion from the two fearless ghost busters, Stephen had managed to bash his elbow whilst trying to grab Jon who was long gone. At last Stephen managed to catch up with Jon in the doorway and for some strange reason they were both laughing. This seemed weird after experiencing such a fright. Jon had hurt his ankle but from the height he had jumped was lucky not to have broken his leg. Neither was sure of what or who had caused this window to crack but on a later visits Stephen again was to have an odd experience in the same room.

The rest of the night passed fairly quietly only enlivened by Paul offering to throw one of the more arrogant team members from another group off the parapets if he wandered into the ongoing séance again. Maybe this threat also quietened the spirits but for whatever reason there was little extra to report that night. A bit of a disappointment given the Keeps reputation but as always there is no way that anything paranormal can ever be guaranteed no matter where you are. Next time the team from NEPUK returned to the Keep they had booked the night for themselves. No sharing with other groups this time. Due to other prior commitments with his bike club Paul could not make this night so the team had no medium for this investigation.

Once set up and sorted Stephen made a beeline straight for the Garrison Room. This was mostly because of what he felt was unfinished business from the time before. Early in the night the team attempted some automatic handwriting. For those not akin with automatic writing you basically relax and put a pen on a bit of paper. You then clear your head and let the pen run on the paper.

From that experiment Jon had drawn some stairs with the name Charles on his notebook. Apart from being very interesting not a lot more was thought of this at the time, though Stephen was also complaining of feeling a bit sick for the first time on an investigation.

After a brief break to see how others were doing in the different parts of the castle four of the team headed back to the Garrison room. Why they were drawn there with the rest of the castle to explore is not really known, but they were. They decided to set up a crude Ouija Board with a glass and some DIY bits of paper with YES and NO on. After a short time the glass began to move. From the speed and intensity the glass was moving it was apparent that this sprit energy was very strong and possibly potentially a bit naughty. Naughty may not be a word that you would as a rule associate with ghosts but it is Stephens term to represent a Spirit whose intentions may not very good. As it happens that representation this time was proven not to be wrong.

The glass was moving quite violently between answers, which was a bit worrying for some of the team. With Jon already having written Charles down Stephen asked out if the spirit with them was that of Charles. The glass at once moved to yes. After much questioning the basics of the story go as follows. Charles said he was a jailor at the Keep. Apparently he used to poison his prisoners over a two-week period. In his time at the Keep he got a servant girl pregnant. He was extremely angry with this and decided to get rid of her with a massive dose of poison. Somehow the poisoned food that was intended for the female was mixed up. Charles received the poisoned one by mistake. He obviously died from this and was not very happy about it. Charles said he was responsible for the window being cracked on the previous visit. The sickness Stephen had felt according to him the same kind of sickness his victims would have felt. When the team had begun on the glass, briefly, Emma came through. You may be saying to yourself `Who is Emma`? Well the answer is to go read the chapter in this book on the Ghost of Emma and the relationship between her and Stephen. But suffice to say there is a unique connection and relationship between the pair and Emma made an attempt to warn the group about Charles. One thing was for sure, Charles wanted to hurt one of the team. How did they know? He told them he did.

Around this time things were going a bit mad with the team. Lee another team member had found himself at the top of the staircase within the Garrison Room. At the top of the stairs is a big iron gate about the size of a normal house door. As Stephen was pushing Charles for answers that he did not want to give Stephen found himself in an argument with the spirit of Charles via the glass. Charles was trying to tip the glass over which was a first and Stephen was just as equally determined not to let that happen, fighting with his finger to keep it down. By now Stephen was daring Charles to do something to him or in the room. Stephen has learned that a good pointer for when things are going to happen is that the glass stops and the temperature drops rapidly. After some further arguing and shouting this is exactly what happened. Everyone could sense something was about to happen and it did. The huge iron door at the top of the stairs, a door that could hardly be moved, slammed shut. As is to be expected the reaction was instantaneous, Lee came hurtling down the stairs taking two steps at a time. Oddly once again during the whole episode the team were laughing, maybe when they should have been running out of there but they stayed put. Sadly after such a build up the door slamming was to be the end of the night as far as activity goes. However as the team were to find out on a later visit it was not the end of Charles involvement and interaction with them.

The next and to date the last visit to the Keep was done with Paul and a mixture of old and new members of NEPUK. Paul had heard of the antics from the previous visit and privately had decided to try and keep a little more control over events this time round. Of course the focus for the team was always going to be the Garrison room and that was after a brief tour of other parts of the Keep, where they ended up. Present at this séance was Paul, Stephen, Jon and Lee.

As they entered the room Paul's psychic guard was up and for some reason his senses were fully charged. Why that was the case soon became apparent. As the others prepared for the séance Paul knew that there was some mischievous and possibly evil energies in the room but for some reason he was unable to focus in on them. The energies were like shadows, always moving and avoiding any contact or communication with Paul. He held his peace and did not mention this to the others waiting to see what developed. As is the rule, Paul was unaware of the history of the location but Stephen had done his research, so he knew that at one time witches had been held in The Garrison Room.

Stephen did say later: "I did not think for one minute that they would come through." When the séance started Paul joined in on the Ouija board, he would not as a rule, so in total there were four people around the glass. The witches or the elusive energies that Paul had sensed soon made their presence felt. Stephen and the others felt it was rather "cool" that they were talking to witches. Paul was less happy at this. It soon became apparent that Jon and Stephen were going to be the main targets for the witches attentions and antics. Paul knew that there was now four witches in the room and they appeared to have spaced themselves out equally around the room. Oddly they confirmed all this to the rest of the group via the glass, Paul had expected them to be devious and not to reveal any information at all. There was one witch behind Jon, one behind Stephen and the other two witches were in different corners of the room. They told the group that they had been hung. That was interesting as most people would have assumed a witch would have been burned, not hung, though apparently this did happen. At this point Stephen was trying to get them to do something, anything to show their presence in a physical way. They did not want to play and it was felt they had their own agenda. What become apparent to the team and to Paul is they wanted to focus on the two senior members of the group. Those people who could see where they were due to having some psychic ability.

Paul was aware, had been since the Wallaw investigation that Stephen had some medium/spiritual abilities. He was also aware that Jon had some spiritual ability but as yet he had not learned how to channel or control it correctly. As the team were talking to the witches they did appear to have some sort of respect for Jon and Stephen, avoided Paul completely but still wanted to hurt the other two any way they could. The witches continued to move around the room and when asked, did try and make people feel their presence. Paul however was keeping the psychic protection at 100% and the witches knew there was little they could do to harm anyone. There was a mental game of chess going on at all times between Paul and the witches. At one point they claimed that there were others with them who were going after other groups in different parts of the Keep, which was quite worrying. Paul felt this was a complete bluff but felt unwilling to leave the group in the Garrison to seek out the others. So he decided to call their bluff and stayed where he was. There were some further challenges and claims from the witches via the glass, but nothing in the way of any physical manifestations. They eventually gave up on whatever mischief they were bent on and left the board, though Paul could still feel their presence on the fringes of his senses.

After the witches had left the board Charles again came through again but not with the same aggression as he had the previous time. Talking to Charles this time posed the team with even more questions. He claimed that he had not been telling the truth about his identity. Apparently he had been at the Keep and carried out some horrible acts but Charles was not his name.

Once again it was not clear if this was a case of a hostile energy playing games or a genuine attempt at honesty. The team were not to find out on that night as activity did fade away for the rest of the night. There were reports from other members of the team of some noises and possible flashing lights in other parts of the Keep mainly in the Great Hall. The conclusion of the night was a last walk around the Keep. In one area, the Chapel, Paul walked in and said that he could smell beer. Paul the guide did say that at one time the area had been used as a brewery. However flicking on the torches the reason for the smell soon became apparent. A spreading pool of urine was running under the door from the outside; no doubt some late night reveller was caught short and did not realise or care where he urinated. There are plans to return to the Keep sometime in 2011 as Paul and Stephen would like to utilise all the experience and knowledge they have built up since their first visits.

When they do there is no doubt that there will be spirit energies waiting and ready to test them.

THE WOODEN DOLL

THE HISTORY

The Wooden Doll, as it is now known, is a public house that stands in North Shields with a commanding view over the river Tyne and the fish quay. The history of many of the pubs in and around the river area of North Shields, are linked to the development of the river and the wealth of the town that depended on that growth. But North Shields was not always the prosperous thriving town it now is. By 1281, it was valued at £200 a year. It was a village of two hundred cottages, and home to a thousand inhabitants. A new trade in sea coal was responsible for a large slice of the wealth, with a cauldron fetching nineteen shillings in London. However, the success of the new community brought it into direct conflict with the older and much bigger town of Newcastle, ten miles upstream.

In 1265, the Mayor of Newcastle, Nicholas Scott, arrived in North Shields with a heavily armed band of men and destroyed a new mill that had just been completed. They also set fire to a number of houses. Afterwards, the Prior of Tynemouth successfully brought a lawsuit against Newcastle, extracting an undertaking from the civic authorities there, not to do it again. But only a brief respite was gained.

Newcastle's burghers felt North Shields was taking business away from them. Having failed to stop their rival by force, they lobbied the King for support, arguing the Prior was siphoning off trade that should be generating taxes for the Crown.

The town of Newcastle felt that North Shields was getting too big for its boots and they lobbied for its influence to be reduced. In 1290 they succeeded and Edward I decreed a series of restrictions on trade in Tynemouth that virtually crippled it, economically, and forbade North Shields to operate as a port.

Significantly, the export of coal from the Tyne was reserved as a right of the Freemen of Newcastle. Over the next hundred years, North Shields practically died, with its annual value falling to less than £17.

By 1750, the bulk of land north of the River Tyne was still farmland. The Priory had long since been reduced to a ruin, but the small village of North Shields clung to the shoreline, a ragged street of cottages and warehouses, in places no more than sixteen feet across, its inhabitants mostly seafarers; fishermen and their families, sailors from every country under the sun. But big changes were about to happen.

There was a huge demand for new ships, as the Industrial Revolution began to power Britain's economy and as a result of the long naval war with France. Shipyards opened up on both sides of the Tyne, specialising in sturdy collier brigs that became standard in the coasting and Baltic trades. By 1762, the shipping trade had doubled. North Shields ship-owners and shipyard proprietors began building large houses, on the bank in Dockwray Square. From this time, the town grew rapidly northwards, into Tynemouth. An 1851 Public Health report condemned the whole area of Hudson Street, as 'very unhealthy' as 333 people living in the immediate area had to share 18 privies (toilets) between them! Much of the area was demolished during local authority slum clearances in the 1960s, and today some new housing stands near to the Wooden Doll, but otherwise it remains somewhat isolated from any neighbouring buildings. The first mention of the pub that is now the Wooden Doll was by local historian Charles Steel in his book 'Inns and Taverns of North Shields', the Kings Head, 103 Hudson Street, North Shields, was first recorded in 1827, and was originally a small pub in a fairly densely populated area of the town. During some renovation work in the 1950s, evidence was found of various tunnels, hidden cellars and stairs which led to the conclusion – probably correctly- that it was once used as a smugglers' hideaway and perhaps also as a refuge from the Press-gangs.

It was altered, with various extensions etc in the 1960s-90s and during the 1990s it changed its name to the Wooden Doll. The land on which it stands, is a high embankment overlooking the Fish Quay, on the junction of Tyne Street and Hudson Street, Very close by stands the original 'high light' lighthouse, which was an important landmark for the navigation of ships into the river. The existing "Wooden Dollie" you will see at the pub is the head and shoulders 'Wooden Dolly.' This has sat outside the pub since the 1980's and is a younger version of the 1958-installed 'Wooden Dolly' which stands in the town's Georgian-built Northumberland Square. An interesting part of the history of North Shields is that of the "Wooden Dollies".

In 1814 the female figurehead of a collier brig was placed at the entrance to Custom House Quay, on Liddell Street, and stood there until 1850, when it was vandalised. A second figurehead was placed on the same spot. The "Wooden Dolly", as the figurehead was known, was used by seafarers as a source of good-luck charms, by cutting pieces of wood from her to be taken with them on voyages.

Eventually the figurehead was defaced beyond repair and after 14 years was replaced by Wooden Dolly No. 3. This remained until 1901 when it was replaced with Wooden Dolly No. 4 in the shape of a fishwife. A fifth Wooden Dolly, also a fishwife, was placed in Northumberland Square in 1958 and still remains there.

In 1992 a sixth Wooden Dolly, was placed where the first four had been, at the entrance to Custom House Quay, and can still be seen there, next to the Prince of Wales public house.

The modern pub has seen many owners on and off over recent times and at one time was famed for its live music, with many local bands starting out on their careers here. Of late it has been closed but rumours are that it is about to reopen again. Let's hope so as the view from the pub over the river and fish quay is worth preserving let alone the thriving business the pub once was.

THE INVESTIGATION

In the early years of ghost hunting Stephen put various press releases out into the local newspapers. It was the hope to generate some interest and attract some new locations. From these press releases the owner of the Wooden Doll pub in North Shields, Tyne & Wear, contacted Stephen. He invited Paul and Stephen along for a pre visit to chat over his ideas. They met on a weekday evening and over a drink, on the house which pleased Paul, the owner outlined his plans. He told them that he wanted to host a night to help raise money for the RNLI. Seeing Stephens article gave him the idea to hold a "ghost hunt" night at the pub. As the pub, as has been said overlooks the river and the fish quay it was the ideal charity. Paul who was a keen sea angler also approved of this. The owner claimed he had also some good contacts with local radio, which would come in handy when promoting the event.

He said that while he had owned and manage other bars in the area, he reeled off a list but not being local to the area they meant nothing to either Paul or Stephen, he had made many good contacts in the media industry. Paul did know that the pub was known as a music venue and did attract some well-known faces; including some ex members of the famed local group Lindisfarne. So it seemed logical that there would be some media interest in the bar.

The owner added he had received lots of interest from the locals for such an event when he suggested the idea and he felt the potential for a great event that would raise lots of cash was high. He also offered do all the groundwork such as getting tickets printed, posters sorted and the ticket sales so all Paul and Stephen would have to do is turn up on the night to organise the attendees who had purchased tickets.

The next order of business was to get a tour of the pub; Paul had already been pacing up and down as he was keen to get a look around. The main surprise was when the owner took them down to the cellar then moved a box of crisps to reveal another hatch, a pretty small hatch. As has been noted in the history the pub has a reputation for one being a haven for smugglers. Now Paul is not svelte and he did wonder if he would get through. But after a little bit of breathing in he managed it. They were met with total blackness, might have been a good idea for our two intrepid ghost hunters to have brought torches, but Paul knew even with the darkness that this was going to be a good location.

After a tour of the rest of the pub, the behind bar area was another area that Paul was drawn to, a date was set for the night. In the build up to the night of the event Stephen was in frequent contact with the owner on issues such as ticket sales and pre event publicity. Stephen received one call to be told by the owner he had been on local radio promoting the event with a view to selling even more tickets. This was great news until he informed Stephen that he had told the radio station members of a well known ghost hunting TV show would be there on the night.

When Paul learned of this he had visions of several hundred rather angry punters being a tad hacked off when they found out that it was in fact two, as yet unknown local lads. Stephen pointed out this to the owner and that of course there would not be anyone from the cast at all on the night, the owner's response was he thought it was ok as he didn't say it was the main cast. People on the night wouldn't know who was who. This information and attitude didn't sit easy with Paul or Stephen but both were committed to helping raise money for a good charity. But it did give a little indication for the tone of the night to come.

Little else was needed now except to wait for the night to come around. On the morning of the event Stephen went through the equipment they were going to take, mainly such things as TV and recorders to allow play back of any footage recorded on video cameras as well as to play the feed from 4 remote cameras they were going to use. Packing that lot into Stephen's car while making sure it was secure and safe from any

81

breakage took a little while but they were soon on route.

Upon on arrival there were quite good-sized crowd waiting. What was evident was that the bar staff had been instructed to sell as many tickets to as many punters as they could. This is the down side with doing ghost nights at pubs, alcohol is available. People of varying degrees of drunkenness were preparing to spend time ghost hunting after the pub closed.

There was a good mix of people; some who Paul could sense were also mediums as well as a smattering of experienced investigators who stood out due to the equipment they carried. However there were also several people who just seemed to have bought tickets so they could remain seated at the bar after closing time.

Stephen had particular concerns about a couple, as the female of the pair appeared to be very drunk with her male partner heading that way fast. She looked a sort of a 60's hippy type with braids in her hair, long flowing skirt and a multitude of bangles.

Not all was going to plan either on the equipment front. Stephen could not get the TV equipment to work and was getting very frustrated. It seemed that despite their efforts there was a lead missing. One of them situations where the conversation was along the lines of "I thought you packed it, no I thought YOU packed it." But the end result of course was no one had packed it.

So the TV idea was scrapped and they moved on to the normal safety advice spiel. This was the first time they had really done this to what was a roomful of total strangers so it was all a little daunting but everyone seemed to listen and no one started to snore. Prior to the night Paul and Stephen had agreed to split the groups into two with one group doing a tour with Paul and the other half with Stephen. This would make it all more manageable plus some areas simply would not have accommodated all the people who were attending as a single group. But when Stephen stood up after Paul's part of the safety talk and told of this plan there was a general exodus to head off with Paul. Not anything to do with Paul's undoubted personal charisma but due to people always assuming that more would happen when the medium was present. Wrongly as it happens as so often spirit energy will chat to the medium and not attempt to make their presence known in any other way. However Stephen shepherded some people back to tour with him and stopped everyone from disappearing.

THE FIRST HALF OF THE NIGHT

For the first part of the night Stephen took his small group to the cellar that they had explored on their first visit. All of his group were by chance women and just as he was about to start proceedings the final girl come down the stairs into the cellar. Stephen had not escaped the woman he had reservations about, the rather drunk hippy chick with the braids in her hair. Here she was descending into the cellar and for some reason best known only to her she had no shoes on.

You needed no psychic ability to know that tonight was going to be an interesting one with such a "character" among the group. Stephen asked the group to spread into a semi circle around the cellar; Stephen as was his habit did not join in the group but stood back to watch for any activity or anyone in distress. Unluckily for Stephen as it was to turn out he was positioned behind the woman with no shoes on.

Stephen started with the usual rote of asking out for spirit activity with a few little responses here and there. Then in the pitch dark he heard the hippy women start asking out. Even in her voice Stephen could hear a slightly hysterical tone and was wondering what was going to come of all this. Thirty seconds later she shouted 'he is behind me and undoing my dress.' She meant the spirit but unfortunately Stephen was also standing behind her and he knew what people would be thinking. At this point someone turned a torch onto the crazy girl, jaws dropped when they saw her standing there in only bra and knickers with her dress around her knees. Luckily for

Stephen one of the other girls pulled her clothes back up and ushered her out of the cellar. So 15 minutes into an investigation he already had a crazy stripper and if she was to be believed also an amorous ghost with fingers nimble enough to loosen button in a trice. It was going to be a long night. Paul in the meantime had taken his group to a table with spectacular views over the harbour and had started to conduct a circle. He had a fair mix of people that he felt were mediums as well as those people who were simply there to see what happened.

While he was preparing the circle he was aware of the presence of a male spirit, dressed in what can only be described as old-fashioned seaman garb. The spirit seemed very interested in the proceedings and did not seem at this time interested in communication with Paul. When Paul mentioned this to the group but without going into too much detail one of the guests also reeled off a description of the man that matched how Paul was seeing him.

At the same time a male guest who was one of the people who seemed only to have bought tickets to stand at the bar all night chimed in with some questions. As it happens this man was in fact a knowledgeable local historian of sorts and while not going into too much detail he did tell of the smuggling history of the pub. Something of course that Paul did know of prior to the night starting, though interesting and no doubt well intentioned Paul was not keen to have the group getting a history lesson at that time. This is simply as any information that would be gathered by him or other mediums on the night would be of little value as it could have simply been prior knowledge. So Paul thanked the man and explained his reasons and thankfully the man subsided.

Paul opened the circle and at once the aforementioned seaman joined the circle. Paul could see that he was standing behind one of the guests, a female and that he appeared to be one of those spirits who enjoyed scaring or teasing people. This was going to be the case as Paul watched as he stooped and blew onto the woman's neck. As the group were holding hands in a circle she merely flinched but he could tell in her eyes that she was wondering if she had really felt that?

Sensing that this man had no malicious intent Paul asked him to repeat the action. This time the woman knew she had felt something and started and glanced around the circle. Paul gently explained what was happening and the woman laughed rather nervously but seemed game enough to want to carry on. So Paul asked the spirit man why he had chosen to tease that particular woman, they were several others around the table, the man answered, "Her hair was like his Lizzie's." Upon questioning him who Lizzie was Paul was told that she was his wife.

The story emerged that this man had lost his life on the other side of the world in a shipping disaster. Not due to a war or any conflict but simply one of the usual hazards of sailing at that time. A huge storm had blown up and a wave had swamped his ship. He had no idea where this had happened as he said that it was only the captain who knew where they were going. Rather oddly though he did not perish at once. He managed to swim away and grab some flotsam to hang on to till the storm blew out.

However, that was the end of his good luck and he drifted for many days as he put it but finally lack of water drove him mad. He decided to simply let go of the wreckage and drown. He claimed his last thought was of those he had left behind. When Paul asked why he came to the pub to see Lizzie the man looked surprised. He said when he was alive this was where he lived and it was then a row of houses. He impressed into Paul's mind a picture of what would now be called a slum. A street of rough cobbles, dirty children with no shoes, dressed in rags with what looked like sewerage flowing down the middle of the street. This the man had said was why he had gone to sea, to try and get himself and Lizzie away from this, but it was not to be.

The man was now very melancholy and was starting to fade; his energy going fast, his last comment was that Lizzie had waited all her life for him before passing over herself at a young age. This man's energy was gone before Paul had a chance to ask why they were not reunited in the spirit world. This tale seemed to have affected all that heard it; even history man was now gazing morosely into his pint. So a break for what Paul hoped would be a soft drink seemed a good idea.

Shortly Stephen and his group rejoined the party and Paul learned of the antics of the woman and her impromptu strip tease. As Stephen was relating the story the said woman was now sitting at the table recently vacated by Paul and his group. She had an empty upturned glass in front of her and appeared to be having her own private Ouija board's session. Even though there was no board or letters in front of her she had her hand on a glass that was whizzing around the table at a frantic speed, propelled of course by her, while she voiced the letters it was going to.

Paul and Stephen decided the best option was to let her carry on while she seemed happy and not disturbing the other guests. Her male partner was still at the bar where he had been when they arrived and was still just resolutely drinking, so again as he seemed happy he was left to carry on with that.

THE SECOND PART OF THE NIGHT

Now it was time for the groups to reverse the locations and Paul was to take his group down the cellar while Stephen stayed above ground with his group. At Paul's suggestion it was decided to hold a séance in the other bar, away from the drinkers and the hippy woman and her invisible Ouija board. Not only for that reason, but also mainly as Paul felt there could be activity in that area.

Paul led his group down into the lower of the two cellars. He had this time brought with him a torch that was equipped with a red filter. So while giving enough illumination to ensure people could move around safely on what was an uneven floor, it was not as bright as to be intrusive. Paul asked all to arrange themselves in a circle and clasp hands, this time he decided to join in the circle and once everyone was in position and happy the light was turned off. As before there was complete and utter darkness. As the group settled Paul opened the circle placing the usual blessing on the area and began to work with the energy of the circle to build momentum or energy. The theory is that spirits can use the energy created in this manner and it allows them to be stronger and give a higher degree of activity in some cases. As Paul was speaking he was aware of a spirit man moving around the outside of the circle. The man appeared to be in his late 20s or early 30s, short and plump. He appeared to be very interested in the activity going on but also a little fearful of interacting or making contact with anyone. As he circled the group at last Paul could see him clearer and it was plain that he would have suffered from Down syndrome when alive. This would explain the oddity of the feeling Paul was getting from him, a masculine energy but yet childlike.

He continued to walk around the outside of the circle obviously fascinated by what was going on and particularly with one of the women who at one point he started to raise his hands seemingly to touch her hair only to withdraw them fearfully. At this point Paul explained to the group what he could see and then spoke directly to the man, asking him his name. It was plain that the man could hear and understand Paul but he simply smiled at him and continued his way around the circle, once again stopping at points to look at the people in the circle. At one of these "stops" the woman he was standing behind asked "is he behind me." Paul assured her he was but that she had nothing to be worried about. The lady concerned said that she was not worried only that she was aware of a feeling of her personal space being invaded.

After a few more minutes of gently questioning at last the man ceased in his circling and started to respond to Paul's questions. To the question again on his name this prompted the response "boy." Paul misunderstood this and replied that he knew that he was a boy, or in fact a man but he wanted to know what he was called, however once again the response was "boy". It appears that in fact this was what the young man used to be called by the men he had worked with and in the end simply took that as being his name. What his real name was or even if he ever had one was not known. The rest of his story emerged of this man living almost all his life inside a house and not being allowed out at any time. He said a woman looked after him, keeping him clean and feeding him but he was unsure or unable to understand if he was his mother. But from his description it was plain to Paul and the rest of the group that while he had not been abused he had not received much in the way of love or tenderness. Only that his physical needs appeared to have been cared for in the way a animal is kept feed, watered and warm with little concern for any other needs. He did say that at one time he had moved a window covering to one side and was looking out on the street where he lived but some other children saw him and began to laugh at him. Pointing and then starting to throw pebbles at the window till shooed away by the woman who then tore him away from the window and told him he must never do that again. He told that a slap around the head that made his ears ring reinforced the message.

This it appeared was his world for quite some time, he had no understanding of weeks, months and years it seemed. Then one day a man appeared and as he put it "took him away." He could not really tell Paul who this man was but what he was able to convey was the utter terror he felt at being suddenly dragged away from the only world he knew and brought to the place he was at now. There he was put to work, his job it seemed started out plainly enough. He had to look after the men he worked with, fetch and carry simple things like their "ale". He appeared to have been treated reasonably well and kindly though still getting the odd cuff around the head from the men when he got things wrong, but again his world was restricted to the place he worked at and his wages seemed to be bed and board. He did say that on most days his board was simply bread unless the other men gave him any leftovers or treats.

However, as he grew older and more importantly stronger it appears that he was given more responsibility and was particularly proud of his strength. He could not really tell Paul in any understandable way what his work consisted off but he did show himself carrying two barrels, one on each shoulder. This it seemed was quite a feat when they were full of some kind of liquid. However he then one day when he woke up and started to work none of the men would speak to him, seemingly oblivious to his speaking to them.

Thinking that he had done something wrong and was being snubbed he was utterly miserable and this went on he said "for a long time." How long that is, it is impossible to say. But he did say that he saw the men come and go and new people he did not know start to work there till one day no one came and he was alone. The man then claimed that was how it had been since then and he still did try to speak to and touch people he saw but they ignored him as well. By now it was clear to Paul that what had happened of course was that the young man had died but somehow had not understood this. Paul asked if the man ever saw the woman that used to look after him and if he did why he did not go with her. The young man said he had seen her a long time ago but did not want to go as he was afraid of doing wrong and leaving where he was working. At last it seems she stopped coming.

Paul gently explained what he thought but it seemed beyond the comprehension of the man. But when Paul explained that he would not "get wrong" if he went with this woman, the young man at last appeared relieved. On Paul gently questioning he agreed that he would go with this woman next time he saw her. Seemingly at that moment a woman appeared next to the man and placed her hand on his shoulder. The look on his face was one of pure joy and he hugged the woman as though he was afraid to let go. The women mentally said to Paul that "I will look after him now," and both she and the young man faded from the atmosphere.

During all this Paul was as best he could relate the events to the rest of the circle. As is to be expected many were deeply affected by the story and the ending. None wanted to continue and try and connect to any other energies so Paul closed the circle and they all ascended back up to the bar area. They found the rest of the group sitting sipping drinks and at first they were shocked to see many of the people in Paul's group red eyed and weepy. But as they paired off into groups the story was told and retold about the man in the cellar.

Paul himself had quick word with Stephen and then took himself away alone to recover himself, he had been physically and emotionally drained by the communication in the cellar but he did say at the end of the investigation that it was one of the greatest moments in his mediumship career, being able to help a poor soul to find comfort and healing.

The next 30/40 minutes passed as a social session with all the people swapping their tales and experiences. Not only of the night but also on other investigations they had been on or in some cases mediums they had received readings from.

THE LAST PART OF THE NIGHT

That turned the conversations around to doing as a finale for the night a group séance. With every member present and with the hope this time that instead of looking for energies within the pubs it would be a more personal experience. With peoples loved ones coming through to them via the Ouija board.

Paul and Stephen's attitude was that "it's your night" and if that is what people would like to do then they are more than happy to do so. The logistics concerned Paul at first as figuring out how to get 22 people around a table and fingers on the glass was daunting. But as it turned out not all wanted to join in, many simply wanted to watch this being their first time. However there were still around 9 people including Paul who was going to around the table. Stephen was going to join those who were observing. So a large table was brought into the room and people gathered around the board. Unfortunately at this time the "hippy lady" who had fallen asleep woke up and wanted to join in. Paul was not happy with this and looking at the faces of others neither were they. However she had paid for her ticket so she was entitled to join in. Now with much more experience under their belts both Paul and Stephen would not have allowed this. But at this time and hoping not to spoil the night there were prepared to allow it. Thankfully before the séance could start "hippy lady's" partner demanded that it was time to go. After a little bit of a spat between them they did leave and Paul observed that they would struggle to get a taxi at this time in the morning. However, as has been said before, the pub had a commanding view of the harbour and a few minutes later the rest of the group saw the couple emerge from what must have been stairs and make their way along the road. What was not good to see was them then climbing into a car and start to drive away. The angle meant it was not possible to see the registration number or there is no doubt that they would have been reported via a phone call to the police.

Thankfully, after watching as they reversed with painful slowness out of the parking space and set off, the group saw a police car come up the hill and just as they disappeared from view they saw the blue light go on as they were pulled over. With that unfortunate incident complete focus again returned to the setting up of the séance. By now other guests had decided that it was time for them to go and the party left had dwindled down to 8 people. This was however a much more manageable number so to some degree that was a blessing.

The séance was started and maybe as everyone was tired and drained or maybe the events with the drunken couple and their car had upset people but whatever the reason there was not much activity from the boards. It also became clear that there was also now a distinct lack of enthusiasm from most of the remaining group to carry on and also the staff wanted to lock up after a hard shift. Therefore after around a further 30/40 minutes the evening was brought to a close.

As people prepared to leave there was a general feeling that all had enjoyed the night and if another was arranged they would attend and tell their friends of it. But it was also felt that for anyone attending there would have to be a no alcohol rule; Something both Stephen and Paul fervently agreed with. So ended a bit of a baptism of fire for Paul and Stephen, they had learned many valuable lessons that were to stand them in good stead for the future. The main one of course being the no booze rule but also that in future they would take charge of their events and run them as they felt was appropriate. To some degree what they did learn on this event has shaped how they run all their events now. Keeping the atmosphere free, easy and relaxed but ensuring that all show respect to the location, the other guests and to the spirit people.

THE SCHOONER INN

THE HISTORY

The 32-room hotel is listed in the Northumberland Tourist Guide as a 17th Century listed Coaching Inn. Records show that it has been the hub of Alnmouth or Alnmouth village for the past 300 years.

The name Schooner derives from a character of sailing ship (using fore and aft sails on more than one mast) first used by the Dutch in the 16th and 17th centuries and then developed in the Americas from the 18th century onwards. Schooners were cargo vessels, capable of both ocean and coastal travel.

Besides being a legitimate trading port, the village of Alnmouth was also a haven for smugglers and vagabonds. In fact one part of the inn itself is said to have been used by smugglers. Such was the reputation of Alnmouth that John Wesley, the founder of The Methodist Church, commented that it was, "A small seaport town famous for its wickedness." Notable persons who have stayed in the hotel include Charles Dickens, Basil Rathbone, Douglas Bader and even King George III.

The history of the hotel is well documented and there are many stories of murders, suicides and massacres. There are various reports of babies being burned alive, murders and treachery and added to all that of course is its renown as a haunted location after being featured on that well known TV show Most Haunted.

The town of Alnmouth itself is a picturesque place with pleasant beaches. Though the town does get very busy in the height of the tourist season and parking in the centre can be a little difficult.

Lately the hotel is in new ownership and a refit of the rooms and a facility has been done. From reports all too good effect so even if you do not want to be haunted it's still a good place to take a break at.

THE INVESTIGATION

This event came about as Stephen wished to hold a charity event in aid of Tommy's. http://www.tommys.org/. This charity funds research into pregnancy problems and provides information to parents. They say, "When a pregnancy fails or a baby dies, the families affected can be devastated and often have a desperate need to know why". This was the case with a friend of Stephen and seeing the distress at the loss of their baby he decided to do something to help.

He set about looking for a venue for a charity ghost hunt, a star guest who would be willing to contribute their time and of course some other willing volunteers to assist him on the night. Paul was more than happy to join in with the planning and to act as the medium on the night.

The first thing to decide was where to host the event. Several locations were considered and discarded for one reason or another till finally The Schooner Inn at Alnmouth was chosen and booked. There were many reasons for this but the location of the inn was a key factor, being reasonably close to Paul and Stephens's hometowns. Plus the reputation of the site after it was featured on Most Haunted was a huge factor and finally the help and kindness of the staff and management when they were told of the reason for the event sealed the deal.

The project was given a tremendous boost when Jason Karl of Most Haunted fame was unhesitant in agreeing to lend his time free of charge to the event. So with everything in place and tickets for the night sold out it was just a case of waiting for the night to come around. As a further twist to the night Stephen had decided to spend the night prior to the event at the inn staying in one of the most haunted rooms, in this case room 28. He had also booked the room for the night of the investigation to ensure access for the guests though he did not anticipate much sleeping going on that night. The day of the event soon came around and Stephen as has been said had already spent the night at the hotel. Friends and guests who were to attend the event soon joined him and later in the afternoon Jason arrived, with Paul due to other commitments not arriving until early evening.

Upon Paul's arrival he found them all sitting in the conservatory part of the bar with soft drinks and coffee in evidence, no alcohol was allowed to be drunk on the night. Once introductions had been made and no doubt names promptly forgotten another pot of coffee was served and plans were made for the night. As it was not a large group on this night plus it was one of the first events that Paul and Stephen had worked together with the public it was agreed that the old maxim of KISS was a good one. Keep It Simple Stupid. There are ruder versions of that but we shall keep it, well simple.

So it was agreed that the whole group would work as a unit for the first part of the night and then later if it was felt that activity, or lack of it made it worthwhile they would split into smaller groups. Once that was sorted the next order of business was of course to pump poor Jason for information about Most Haunted. He didn't really think he was going to get away with out that did he?

Though fully aware that staff members on that show have to sign a confidentially agreement as part of their terms and conditions, the rest of the group did hope for some juicy gossip. Sadly it was not to be and Jason was professional as always. Though he did have high praise for the then star of the show, Derek Acorah and defended him against the allegations of cheating and prior knowledge that was in the news at the time. By now the time had reached 8pm and Stephen had arranged with the Schooner for a buffet meal to be served in the rear of the restaurant in a private room, so all the team headed for the food. It was soon apparent that the Schooner had been very generous in the amount of food that they had provided, way more than could be eaten by the team even if they grazed all night in between vigils, so plates of sandwiches, pies and such like were dispatched to the bar to be shared among the regulars. While munching on the excellent food and chatting a couple of the staff of the Schooner Inn joined the group. While they were there they mentioned an item they had on E bay being auctioned for charity. It was jokingly known as "A ghost in a bottle." In fact what it was of course was simply a large empty bottle in which smoke had been blown into the bottle sealed. But it did sell quite well, mainly they said to the American market and cash was being raised for a good cause. Jason mentioned that he had seen the item on E Bay and had bid but had not been successful. At once the Schooner offered to give Jason a bottle that he was delighted to accept but insisted on making a donation to the charity to the value that was usually achieved on E Bay. Another good cause being supported, the night was going well and the main event was yet to start.

By now word had spread in the hotel that another ghost hunt team was on an event but more interesting there was a star of TV among them. Once the news was known and the regulars in the bar knew who it was, it was pretty obvious that Jason was going to be signing a few autographs. So he with the rest of the group behind him, made their way to the bar. Once there, as expected, there was quite a crowd interested in chatting to and meeting Jason.

As this was as a charity event Jason and the regulars were great. He was more than happy to meet people and sign autographs as well as having his photo taken with people but he did ask that people made a contribution to the charity. An empty bucket was soon found and passed around the bar and thanks to the generosity of the people there it was soon filling up with cash. But after an hour or so of working the crowd, who were getting increasingly boisterous as more alcohol was consumed, Jason insisted that we had to get on with the main part of the night, the ghost hunt. The base for the evening was Stephens's room, which as has been said, was also billed as one of the most haunted. However it was agreed that first it would be a good idea to carry out a tour of the hotel to try and fix the layout in people heads ready for the evening ahead.

The Schooner is perhaps typical of buildings of this age in that it at first it appears to be a bit of a rabbits warren, making navigation for the unfamiliar a little difficult. But after a slow walk around and some direction from Stephen who had spent parts of the previous night investigating the layout was at last fixed in people's heads.

THE CELLAR

The first place that was chosen to go was the cellar. Thankfully unlike many pub cellars this one had easy access down a set of steps. Like most cellars though it was dark, dank and damp. The floor of the cellar is paved with cobles and it is said that they are the originals from when the inn was built in the 17th century.

It is also said that there is a tunnel that leads from the cellar direct to the sea. Smugglers used this in olden times to evade the prying eyes of the authorities, though the team could not see any evidence of that. The team found a place to sit wherever they could and torches were switched off and the vigil began. The first thing that was noticed was the absolute darkness. Rarely do most people actually encounter a situation where they really cannot see their hands in front of their faces. But this is how it was for the team.

As ears and eyes adjusted to the environment but did little to penetrate the dark, Stephen took the lead and began to ask out for evidence of any spirit presence. There was little reaction though some people thought they saw some orbs. Paul was of the opinion that as he could feel absolutely nothing that there was nothing there. One slight bit of excitement was caused when one team member said he could hear a tapping noise from the outside wall but that was traced quite quickly to a water drip. The group spent a further 10 minutes in this location again asking for some sort of evidence of any spirit presence but again with no result. So either Paul was right or the energies did simply not want to play tonight.

Whatever the reason it was a disappointing start to the night as Stephen had expected activity in the cellar based on reports he had read from other groups who had visited that area. As by now time had moved on and the bar area had cleared of drinkers it was decided to hold a séance in this area. Stephen as usual had done his research on the Schooner and assured the team that there was tales and history connected to this area and he would be interested to see what, if anything happened.

THE CHASE BAR

The Schooner Inn has 2 bars, this one and the other called, The Long Bar. The Schooner's staff had not long finished clearing and cleaning the bar after the night drinkers had left. However it still had the smells of all bars then, beer and stale tobacco smoke, smoking at the time was still legal in a bar. As the group entered the bar and began to gather chairs around a table in preparation for the séance using a Ouija board Paul was aware of a young spirit girl standing silently observing the group. She looked to be about 7 to 8 years old to Paul's untutored eyes and seemed simply curious as to what was going on. Looking at her clothes Paul thought she was working class and at first she appeared to be a normal looking pretty child, then as he observed her she turned her face to him and it appeared to briefly metamorphose into the same face but it was heavily burned and bloody. This burning only seemed to be affecting her face though. Paul could see her neck and it looked in his words "normal." The appearance to be frank was stomach churning and Paul was glad when the effect faded and once again there was a normal looking small child standing in front of him. After recovering from the shock of this transformation Paul attempted to communicate with the young girl, sending out a mental "hello." However at his first attempt the young girl shied away and turned and skipped away, seemingly unafraid of Paul but not wanting to "chat."

By now the preparation for the séance was completed, Paul was surprised to see that his focus on the young girl had not been noticed. He decided to say nothing to see if by chance this little girl used the board to contact the group. The group settled and Paul did his usual preparation with protection and blessing on the group the one of the guests began the usual rote of asking for any spirits persons to make contact or show themselves.

For the first 5/7 minutes or so there was no reaction then there was a slight tremor from the glass before it again fell still. After another few minutes the glass again started to tremble and then slowly move. Seemingly at first at random moving to all corners of the board and at times simply circling the letters. Paul explained that in fact this was quite common and the person trying to communicate was simply looking at and learning the board. As he finished that sentence the glass for the first time move quite strongly to "Yes." So it was plain that whichever spirit person was coming through on the board could also hear the group, or at least Paul.

Further questioning was at first very confusing, as the answer to the questions, "Are you a man or woman" both received a yes answer. After a little further questioning what became plain was this was a family group with both a male and a female in it. It also appeared that at times differing energies were using the glass to communicate as strange as it may seem the group soon noticed a difference in how the glass was being moved. One energy was much more "direct" while another appeared to be more hesitant in the replies and the way the glass was moved, often having long pauses before answering a question so at times guests around the table repeated or rephrased the question. Which again often give rise to confusion as to which questions were being answered. However after a period of time some clues to who was coming through started to emerge. It appeared there were a man and a woman who were partners, man and wife, but had crossed over separately, not just in time but also in distance.

The man told of an accident that had killed him, he simply said that "the sea had got him" but it was not clear how this occurred. Other than he was at pains to point out that he was not at fault. The female half of the pair was very concerned about her children; again it seemed that one of them had died young in an accident. Once again there was no clue to what the accident was but again she also was very strongly saying that it was not her fault. During all this Paul had not mentioned the young girl that he had seen when he entered the bar but at this point he asked, "Was she burned?" The glass shot to yes and if it is possible to transfer emotion through such an inanimate object as a glass then this is what happened. The glass appeared to be vibrating or shaking extremely quickly and for several minutes it simply stayed at Yes while shaking. After a little while further Paul began to ask questions of this woman and her tale slowly emerged. It seemed that somehow, it was impossible to find out how, the young girl Paul had seen had fell into a fire and the picture of a burnt face that Paul had seen was the result. The woman on the glass was her mother and it was still obvious despite her claims she felt at fault for the accident. She did say that now mother and daughter were together in the spirit world and happy but she still felt pain at the agony her daughter had experienced as a result of the burn. As the energy faded from the glass and its movement grew weak Paul did ask for this woman to tell the group her name, either through the glass or through Paul. The last letters spelt out were L and Z. It was not possible to find out any further information so it is not clear what those letters indicate. They of course could be initials but who's the group had no clue. The whole séance had been very emotional and it was universally agreed that a short break was in order and maybe a coffee. The group returned to the base room, Stephens's bedroom Room 28.

ROOM 28

As has been said before this is, one of the rooms within the hotel was labelled as the most haunted, though Stephen, as reported did spend the previous night there with his partner. There have been reports of screams being heard in the room, raps, clicking noises and dark shadows being seen. Some people who have stayed in or visited the room also complained of feeling unwell, dizzy, sick and very uneasy. But Stephen reported a night of uninterrupted sleep. The plan had been to leave this room till last, given its reputation but the fact that everyone was now in there seemed too good a chance to miss. This time rather than hold a séance it was agreed to simply hold a vigil, for everyone to at first sit quietly to observe and listen for any type of activity. Therefore everyone found a comfortable spot to settle down in and the lights were turned off.

Paul had positioned himself near the rear of the room and had a good vantage point being able to see around 95% of the room. As always people were asked to wait some time to allow their eyes to adjust to the darkness. A useful exercise for anyone to do when on investigations as not only does it help with night vision but it also gives everyone a chance to chill out and relax a little. In both Paul and Stephen's experience it is when people are relaxed and not expecting anything that things do tend to happen. Would it be the case tonight?

There was nothing to report for about 15 minutes or so and to be honest as it was early morning by now Paul felt there was a good chance of people falling asleep. The room was warm, cosy and throw in the darkness then this was a strong possibility. But just as Paul's mind began to drift a little he thought he saw a dark shadow sidling along the wall next to the door. But as his mind had been elsewhere so he discounted it as just possibly passing cars headlights. Though to be honest at this time in the morning he had not noticed any traffic. However as he waited he started to sense the presence of a man now standing near the foot of one of the beds, the one nearest the door. He was more a dark shadow then a visible presence but Paul could feel the strong masculine aura he was giving off. Paul attempted to communicate with this male energy but he was soundly ignored. He knew the man could "hear" him as Paul did sense him turn to look at him but then turn away. This male energy seemed to be focused on one of the female guests who were sitting on the foot of the other bed. In fact focused would put it mildly; the attention he was given this women was intense.

Since he was refusing to communicate with Paul added to the unease Paul felt with this man Paul maintained his full focus on him. He also made sure that he sent out a continuous stream of thoughts aimed at the man warning him that Paul would react if he attempted to harm this woman or any of the other guests. In all this Paul's was also aware of both smelling and tasting blood. He had the metallic taste in his mouth very strongly. What this was he was not sure but he did feel it was not as a result of an injury, more a case of being spattered with blood that splashed onto the face and mouth. At last Paul stream of warnings seemed to have an effect and the man turned his focus on Paul, the intensity and malevolence of the stare was startling. Though privately concerned, Paul simply attempted to maintain a cool and unconcerned outer appearance. There was no doubt though in Paul's mind that this man was not only capable of but had taken a human life. This seemed to work as Paul sensed an easing in the intensity as well as a slight feeling of concern slipping into the male energies thoughts, as though he was now slightly worried that his intimation tactics had not worked.

At this point the women who had been the focus of this energies attention suddenly asked, "Is someone staring at me?" There was a general negative response from the other guests so Paul asked the women why she had asked the question. The answer was that she felt as if as she put it: "The same as when you get some creepy guy watching you." which was interesting, as Paul had not shared the presence of the male energy with anyone in the room.

Deciding to continue with this theme Paul asked the lady what her response would have been to such a stare if it happened. The women's reply was a little fruity to record here, but suffices to say that she would have a "frank and open exchange of views with such a man." Oddly at this the male energy seemed to bridle, as though he had been verbally attacked himself, even though the words were not aimed at him. He appeared to make to take a step towards the woman and Paul again sent out a warning thought which stopped him in his tracks. The male energy again turned to face Paul and then simply vanished. Paul could no longer see him nor could he sense his presence.

However, a few moments later there was a loud sharp rap or crack at the window. Of course everyone jumped and there was a couple of screams but since a gale was developing outside after a brief discussion it was agreed that that could have been the cause of the knock.

The group again settled down and again almost at once that quiet had taken over one of the guests sitting at the head of one of the beds said he could hear a scraping noise. No one else at the time could hear this but as the minutes passed it became clearer. The sound appeared to be coming from the wall that adjoined the next room and was a slow but steady scraping sound, as though fingernails were being slowly dragged across wallpaper or wood. After a few more minutes of this Paul asked if there was an energy present would they like to make themselves known, unfortunately this had the effect of stopping the noises.

Despite several more attempts the noise did not reoccur. So again everyone settled down to see if anything else would happen. After a further few minutes, one of the guests asked the usual question heard at these events: "Did you hear that?" Another guest who was seated on a chair near the door to the room asked, "Do you mean the kids?" It seemed that they could hear what they felt was the faint sound of young child; they were not sure of the gender, crying, wailing as if in pain.

The guest nearest the door stood and opened the door but nothing could be heard and others agreed the noises had stopped. It seemed tonight the group were being treated to the full gamut of activity within the room but none wanted to develop into any kind of full-blown activity. A little frustrating but that is the nature of ghost hunting, nothing can be predicted. It was agreed to again sit quiet and hold another vigil to see if room 28 had anything more to give.

This time the response was immediate, there was a series of loud raps or knocks from the same adjoining wall that the scratches had came from. Once again the group attempted to communicate with whatever was causing the noise but was unsuccessful. They asked for the noise to be repeated and it appeared that whoever or whatever was the cause would wait till just before everyone patience was about to run out before giving a few more sharp knocks. As though to simply tease the group. Even when Stephen spoke out and said if the energy did not wish to communicate then the group would leave and it would have no one to tease there was no response. So after a further wait of about 10 minutes that is what the group decided to do. As one of the bedside lights was switched on there was another but far louder and violent crash on the window. This time everyone did jump and most felt there was no doubt that some type of energy was expressing disapproval for some reason. The group did stand and wait for a short time to see if there was going to be a follow up to the crash but none was forth coming, even when one of the guests taunted whoever caused it to repeat the noise.

So even though there had been some activity in the room it was decided to head off to other parts of the hotel that Stephen wanted the group to visit. However as they left the room Paul indicated he wanted to spend a little more time in the area around this room. Most of the group headed downstairs for a quick coffee break before the next vigil but two of the guests stayed with Paul.

The reason that Paul wanted to stay a little longer in the area was that as the group left room 28 he was also aware of a spirit energy pushing past them and heading down the corridor. This energy though very fleeting in contact he felt was female. Paul made his way away from room 28 and soon encountered the female energy. She again flew by Paul heading once again for room 28 seemingly aware of Paul but so engrossed in her business as to ignore him. The two guests with Paul exclaimed that they had felt a rush of wind or a draught. They of course did not know the reason for this, but they were adamant that they both had felt it. Paul noticed that the female energy was again heading back towards him and this time she stopped and looked around her, the agony and terror in her gaze was heart breaking to see. This time she acknowledged Paul's presence and he heard muttering or a continuous babble coming from her. Although very difficult to make out the stream of words without any breaks, as would be present in normal speech, Paul was able to piece together a little of what she was saying. Her most common phrase was that she was "a good wife." She was also babbling about her "bairns," her boys, and it seemed that she was concerned about the children that harm had come to them. Someone had hurt them and though she was aware that she was now a spirit and had crossed she seemed to be reliving an event that occurred while she was alive. As she appeared to be almost incoherent with fear and worry there was little more that Paul could make sense from verbally. But the emotions emanating from her was of having experienced an ordeal so terrifying that it would still cause her to relive it and there was no doubt in his mind that other people would have seen or felt this woman while staying at the hotel. He also felt that somehow this was also connected to the man he had seen in room 28. The woman faded from Paul's mind and the corridor was empty, though Paul had been recounting what he was seeing and hearing to the two other guests they had neither seen nor felt anything further since the draught they had first encountered. So it was decided to join the rest of the guests for a coffee.

105

Back downstairs over some excellent coffee the guests were examining a gadget that had been sent to Jason to test. For want of a better description let's call it a "ghost detector". It consisted of a hand held box that was about palm size. On it there were 4 lights of differing colours arranged in a square pattern. The basic idea was they indicated which way to go, forward left, right as the top light lit, ditto to reverse and if both lights lit it was straight forward or back. Basic to operate but of course how it worked or if it worked was unknown.

There were two further areas that Stephen had planned for the group to investigate. So Jason decided to give the gadget a go at the next location within the hotel. Paul kept his own opinions to himself, which might have been a first for Paul but privately he was scornful of the gadget. However Stephen, ever the gadget freak, was quite interested in the little device. They both were interested to see how it would perform "out in the field" so to speak. That "field" was to be a corridor outside room 17. As always Stephen gave no reasons to the group for his choice of location.

ROOM 17 (THE CORRIDOR)

As they approached this area Paul was conscious of a squeaking noise coming from it. An odd noise to hear in the dead of night in a small seaside hotel as it sounded like the squeal of a rusty cycle wheel as it turned. Jason had his gadget turned on but thankfully the sound turned off and the lights were indicating to continue straight ahead. Paul who was in the middle of the group was by now getting seriously hacked off at the noise and commented that whoever was making it would be very unpopular with any other hotel guests. Only to be met with blank looks from the rest of the group. It dawned on him that what he was hearing was in fact paranormal activity. As Paul does not as a rule receive information audibly he was a little surprised himself. But it soon became obvious to him who and what was causing the noise as he saw a young spirit boy pedalling an old fashioned tricycle for all he was worth towards

106

the group. He seemed determined to hit one of them but stopped short when Paul sent out a "hello" to him. He seemed surprised to be able to be seen but once over that shock he reverted to the being a typical young boy caught doing something he should not by an adult, both looking a little fearful but with defiance in his manner. Interestingly Jason's ghost gadget had stopped flashing and all four lights were steady which it appears indicated that there was a ghost "here." Paul in all this had not told of his meeting with the ghost boy so he was again surprised to find that the machine was in this case accurate. Paul resumed his chat with the young lad, or tried to as he had now decided to go shy on Paul. But what emerged was an explanation of what the young lad was up to. It seemed that he hated being ignored, as I suppose does any young child when seeking attention. So he had took to riding his tricycle up and down the corridor, Paul could not find out why this corridor, and when hotel guests who of course could not see him ignored him he took to banging into doors and walls. He also claimed that he would use the handlebars of the trike to scrape the walls and doors to leave marks so people could see he had been there. Paul did try to get more information from the young lad to ascertain his name, why he was there and when and how he had died. But each time he attempted to get such information a sullen face and a refusal to speak from the young boy met him.

After a pretty short period of time Paul got the impression that this young lad was growing bored with speaking to this grown up and just wanted to continue to play. So Paul simply asked if he wanted to play tricks on the rest of the group, where upon the young lads face changed into one of a mischievous glee. Paul asked the young lad to do something to let the people around him know that he was there as only he could see and hear him. With impish delight the lad set off towards the group and just before hitting them he veered and crashed into the wall. All the guests heard the resulting knock, stopped what they were doing and stared at the spot where the young lad was sitting beaming at Paul.

Upon Paul grinning back, the young lad waved and then disappeared from sight, though Paul could still sense his presence on the fringe of his psyche. He told the rest of the group the tale and what the young lad had done to get attention. They of course wanted a repeat but despite several of them at various times asking for the young lad to do it again" the boy and his tricycle never reappeared. As by now time was, as it always does, marching on and while Stephen had booked rooms for those that wished to stay many guest faced a long drive it was decided to move on to the next location as suggested by Stephen.

ROOM 23

This was not billed as the most haunted room, room 28 as has been said takes that honour, but it is said that this area also has lots of activity. Paul briefly broke away from the rest of the group. He as he said wanted to "take a psychic shower," which means to cleanse himself of all of the psychic energy that he had picked on during the night. So he was a little late in joining the rest of the group because of this and also as he freely admits he also got lost in the maze that is the Schooner. When he did they were preparing for a séance using the Ouija board in room 23. Paul as was his habit opted to simply observe and did not take a place at the board.

The usual preparations were made and though he was not taking part Paul still did his normal blessing and cleansing of the room prior to starting. Light were turned off though a small battery lantern was allowed to stay on to better see the board, it also made any filming easier as not all the guests were around the board, some were using their camera phones to record. As a rule the Ouija board is not a tool that you get an instant response with. It seems that most of the time any spirits need time to build up energy and as has been said before to learn the board. This time however there was an immediate response when the question "is there any spirit energy wishing to speak with us", was asked. The glass shot to "Yes" and back to the

108

middle of the board ready for the next question. It seems there was an experienced board player coming through. The usual questions were asked with regard to name and dates etc. The name given was William but the date was incomplete. It started with 184 but after then it appeared that the energy through the glass was unsure. What did come through was that this energy was angry and felt it had been shown in a bad light at the time of his crossing. William claimed he was murdered in the hotel and it was "the big bugger" that did it. He said add that "the lass" helped his murderer in the crime. He was very insistent that he had been wronged and that he should have got justice even though he had died, he still even now of course crossed over felt his killer should be facing justice.

As has been said Paul was not taking part in the séance but from where he was standing he could see in the dim light the door handle was slowly moving. As though someone outside was trying to make a stealthy entrance to the room. He called out: "Is that you outside William?" The glass shot again to "No," but the handle stopped moving. For some reason Paul had a feeling that this William was not telling the full story of his demise and starting to question him. Oddly even though Paul was voicing out loud the questions the answers were coming via the board. When asked "why was he murdered" at first there was no response, the glass stayed resolutely still. Only when Paul began to make random suggestion to the reasons did he manage to hit the mark. Paul had asked if William had been killed in a fight. That question provoked a response, but not at first any answer simply that the glass seemed to take of a mad energy and whizzed around the board making no sense. After a while it did calm down at Paul's urging and the board was used to spell the word "fun" repeatedly, which was an odd word to use in the context of a death and a fight. When Paul asked why was it fun the board rather haltingly and with some errors spelt out "with the lass, it was only fun."

After some more probing, where getting information was like drawing back teeth, another story was dragged out of William. It appeared that he while drunk had attempted to force his attentions on one of the staff in the hotel. It was assumed a barmaid and some other male had come across the encounter. During a fight it emerged that William had fallen down some stairs and died. Though he claimed that when the "polis" found his body it was not where it died. The group could not be sure, as William did not say but the assumed that the body had been moved.

William even though after recounting this tale was obviously to blame at least in part for his death still maintained, or felt his death was all a set up and no one seemed really bothered to find out who killed him. By now both Paul and the rest of the group were growing weary of William constant complaining and started to be a little more aggressive in their questions. This did not go down well with William and he seemed to reserve particular fury when any woman doubted his replies and attacked him. The glass at these times seemed to fly around the board and was incapable of settling anywhere and giving a reply.

During one of these sorts of questions when the glass was particularly animated there was a loud and much unexpected bang on the room door. There was one of the guests sitting by it so within a few seconds he had stood and wrenched it open. There was of course nothing and no one there.

The door was closed again and the session on the board resumed. But now it appeared that William had gone there was no response to the questions no matter what they were. An attempt was made to seek out any other energy in the room and there appeared to be a half hearted response to questions but the only response to the question of: "Who are you?" was a weak and laborious spelling out of Ric and Mag. But after that the glass stayed still and nothing further was to come from it. Though as the group were closing the board down and thanking

110

the spirits that came through there were several distinct creaks from the corridor outside the room. As though someone was walking slowly along the corridor but not making any attempt to be quiet. Once again after a few minutes of listening to this the door was opened but with the same result as after the knock, no one was there. So that is this group's experience of the Schooner Inn.

All of the guests felt that there was no doubt that the inn was haunted, though some had heard claims that there was supposed to be 600 ghosts there and felt that was an exaggeration, but all said during the debrief later that they often had the feeling of being watched, not just doing their time in areas during vigils and séances but even while eating the buffet or having a coffee. They were almost evenly split 50/50 on the question: "Would you sleep here?"

The last thing to report on this investigation was that Stephen and his partner spent the rest of the night in room 28 and another guest decided to stay in room 23. They all next day reported they had slept like logs with no disturbances of any kind. So it appears that guests can enjoy a restful night at the Schooner unhampered by paranormal activity. But I wouldn't put the family silver on that bet. Lastly of course, this was a charity event for a very good cause. The night raised over £550. Many thanks to all that gave their time and support.

KIELDER CASTLE

Kielder Castle is set in Northumberland at the head of Kielder Water in the North West of Kielder Forest. The area itself is only three miles from the Scottish Border. Therefore, some of the earliest records talk of how the area suffered border raids and warfare for many centuries. William Wallace's army rampaged through Kielder in 1297 and Robert the Bruce 'laid waste to Keildir' between 1311 and 1312. For defence, the very wealthy built castles. The clansmen generally built Pele towers while the small farms had bastles for defence. The Castle is well placed precisely in the junction of two rivers to catch the right combination of hill, valley and water.

Kielder Castle as it is now was actually a hunting lodge for the Dukes of Northumberland and in the 12th Century, the Scottish kings hunted on the fells in Donkleywood near Kielder. The Duke and Earl Percy had been making regular shooting trips to Kielder before work actually started on the Castle in 1771. Earl Percy and William Newton designed the Castle. Newton was probably Northumberland's leading architect at the time but no doubt, it was still a feather in his cap to land such a project from an esteemed member of the local gentry.

By 1787, there were nine keepers at Kielder, an indication of its importance as a base for hunting. In 1827, the prolific Scottish historic novelist Sir Walter Scott visited Alnwick Castle. Scott had written previously that in 1765 Lord Percy went to shoot game at Kielder and he had been appalled by the behaviour of the tenants. It was told that the women were wearing next to nothing and the men were savage. The females would sing and the men would dance around. Further development continued at Kielder and by 1828, a bridge had been built over Kielder River.

In 1847, the 4th Duke inherited the Castle and then in 1850 major alterations were carried out. The 5th Duke George Percy Died in 1867 and with the death of the 8th Duke in 1930

47,000 Acres of the estate was sold to the Forestry Commission in 1932. In 1945, Kielder Village was built and then extended in 1960. In 1990, Kielder Castle was converted into a visitor centre.

Stephen stumbled across Kielder Castle back in September 2004. He had been searching locations to investigate and sent a speculative email off as he had to a number of possible locations. Surprisingly quickly, he received an email explaining how the Forestry Commission at the Castle were very interested in the idea of the group spending the night. It would fit in well with Halloween activities they were planning themselves. He arranged to go to meet staff on a weekend. It is a 90-minute drive from his home and as he worked full time, weekends were his leisure time. During the week leading up to the meeting, Kielder staff informed Stephen that two local newspapers wanted to publish an article about the proposed stay. Unfortunately, for him due to scheduling conflicts this meant two long drives to Kielder as the two papers wanted to meet him on two different days.

When he did arrive at Kielder Castle and saw it in the "flesh" so to speak he did think, "Expected it to be bigger." Nevertheless, it looked like it would be a great location. Being a visitor centre the Castle was quite busy but he met up with the local press photographer, who had already scouted out and found the location he wanted to use for the picture with Stephen. In one of the downstairs rooms, three mannequins have been dressed and staged to show a typical scene from an era. Two of the mannequins are dressed as Dukes and the other is of a woman sewing. The photographer asked Stephen to strike the same pose as one of the Dukes and go eyeball to eyeball with him. This was very amusing to the public who were visiting the Castle but Stephen being the trouper he is carried on and the shot was obtained to the photographer's satisfaction.

The following day it was a different press photographer. Stephen explained to him the set up used for the previous photo and of course, this photographer wanted to do something different. Stephen no doubt thought he had avoided another embarrassing photo shoot, until the photographer disappeared and returned with a white sheet and a pair of glasses. Stephens' wife of the time thought this was hilarious until she realised it was she going under the sheet and wearing the glasses. To make things more embarrassing the photographer wanted the shot taken outdoors in a wooded part of the grounds.

His plan was to have a bespectacled "ghost" appearing from behind a tree where Stephen was standing with him looking into the camera lens. Stephen did later comment, "I don't think visitors could believe what they were seeing or if it was real". There was now a three-week wait until the night at Kielder so in the lead up Stephen indulged himself in one of his favourite hobbies, some research on the ghost stories surrounding the location.

He could only find two paranormal stories relating to the Castle. The first, of a servant girl called Emma who died of a broken heart. Her lover set off to fight in the Boer War but never returned. There are reports of her being seen walking between the parts of the castle and the well that serviced the Castle. There is a plaque on the well telling the story of Emma. (There is more to add to this story from details that emerged during the investigation) Secondly, was the story of a Fredy (an officer in German Border Police) and a woman called Emine, his girlfriend. They had always wanted to spend the night in a haunted location and got their chance one night at Kielder Castle. The set their sleeping bags up in one of the downstairs rooms and had dozed off. The tale is told that Fredy said, "We had not been asleep long when Emine woke me up saying she could hear a noise. I told her it was the door but I realised I had already closed them all. I have never heard a noise like it." Emine said, "I am too young to die, please let me sleep in the car." Fredy decided they should stay a bit longer but then the room temperature dropped for about 40 minutes. They were surrounded by voices that were neither male nor female; they were also the noises of shuffling feet and the sound of a door being forced open. As the witching hour struck, the couple could stand no more and fled to the safety of nearby streetlights. They spent the rest of the night bundled up in their car and the next day Fredy said, "I won't ever go back there after dark again. What a crazy night!"

THE FIRST INVESTIGATION

Leading up to visit Stephen had assembled a group of friends who were to be staying the night with him. Some had been on investigations before, others were just interested and a few just didn't believe in the paranormal at all. At this first investigation of Kielder, Paul and Stephen had not met so this night is as described by Stephen.

"With all the hype leading up to the stay with the press etc, all I hoped for was that the night was not a total flop. When we arrived, it was just starting to get dark. There are no houses or streetlights near so it literally gets pitch black. One part of the Castle no one else in the group had seen was the attic. I had previously visited this through the day when I was on the photo shoot. This area comprised of two small rooms at the front of the castle that lead into two larger rooms. This area was said to be the servant's quarters. To add to the atmosphere of the night these rooms were filled with lots of old items from the castle, farming equipment, and old pictures etc. Plus maybe best of all some props that were going to be used for the Castles Halloween activities. Finally, to give us a genuine 'haunted castle' feel we also had the resident bats to contend with as they roosted in the larger rooms.

We set up a base in one of the second floor rooms then split into small groups and set off to carry out vigils in various parts of the castle. My group and I settled into one of the rooms at the rear and started asking aloud for any spirits to make their presence known. This normally results in knocks, bangs or other types of noises.

However, this time no matter what we said and no matter how quiet we remained nothing seemed to be happening. My worst fears were starting to come true. I had been building this place up for weeks and the whole night looked as though it was going to pass without any activity. You should never assume there would be activity at any location but by this time, the doubters in the group were rubbing their hands in glee. I was starting to feel the night was going to end with me having a red face and having to eat my words.

Just before midnight feeling a little despondent, I decided to have a lie down across two chairs and was quite prepared to call it a night. A small group had sat themselves over a stairwell and was conducting a séance. I couldn't hear what they were saying but I was aware that they were there. They had also set up some motion sensors behind them. The sensors work by placing two sensors facing each other across an area such as a corridor and if something breaks the beam an alarm sounds. From a distance, I thought I heard the sound of the alarm going off. This was closely followed by what sounded like a herd of elephants as five people went racing past where I was lying. I followed them into a nearby room to find them all out of breath. After they recovered themselves a little, they all started to babble at me at once. At last, I got them to calm down and tell me what had happened. They said whilst conducting the séance they had been asking for spirit activity. In response to this questioning the sensors alarm sounded. The shock of the noise made them all leap off their seats and scramble for safety.

I decided at that this point to use an Ouija Board to see if this would generate any further activity. I say Ouija Board but in this case, it was simply an old table, four bits of paper and a glass. Two bits of paper had YES written on and the other two NO. There was a reason we used two of each response. We have found that if you only have one NO and YES and the answer is the same twice, then the glass keeps pushing the same bit of paper, which can be confusing. It sounds a bit complicated but experience has shown that we get better result using this format.

The normal way in how to use the board is to ask aloud for any spirit energies present to move the glass to show they are present; hopefully the glass will start to move. This time the glass did start to move straight away, so to get some idea of who was moving it we began to ask questions. With only having yes or no for answers you have to think carefully about the questions you are asking, you need to ask questions that can be answered with "Yes" or "No" (there is little point asking complicated questions that require complicated answers.) The first person to come through on the board was one of the Dukes. We devised a novel way of finding out which Duke it was. On the main stairwell and top landing there are pictures hung of the Dukes. One unlucky person was dispatched to the top of the stairs where the rows of pictures start. This area was some distance from where the séance was being held and was in complete darkness. This person, prompted via radio, would slowly move along and shine their torch at each picture in turn. When the torch lit up the correct duke, the glass would point to yes, at which point, we would call over the radio for the person to tell us the portrait of which duke they had the torch pointed at.

A unique method of communication that only seemed to occur at Kielder was that when one spirit had done with talking to us the glass would move to the centre of the board. It would then stop for a moment and then begin to circle the table; it felt as though the new energy was looking the board over to get a feel for where things were before it started to answer our questions. This movement occurred three times on my first night at Kielder. During the rest of the Ouija board session that night two more Dukes, one of which was not happy we were there and Emma the servant girl communicated with us via the board. I think we had all hoped Emma would come through so were all quite excited when she did.

117

One thing that was apparent when communicating with Emma via the Ouija was how much the temperature would change. For example I would also ask her to spin the glass and the temperature could be felt to drop. Then I when would ask her to go and make some noises in a different room. The glass would stop spinning and the temperature would increase. However, we could all sense when she returned due to how cold it would get. On this first visit to Kielder, we think she was responsible for three things. Firstly, a single ceiling light flashed in the adjoining room; secondly, she could be heard whistling and lastly, you could hear her running up the stairs to the attic. She had told us she was running up the stairs to the first room on the left as this was her room. Stephen already knew from his research that this was her room so it was easy to get her to move the glass to yes as he went through a list of rooms.

One other strange thing was that she could see the room we were sitting in carrying out the séance both as it was now but also as it was when she was alive. She could also see items on the table we were using but because they had not yet been invented when she was alive, she did not know what they were. After that first night, we all left with mixed emotions."

THE SECOND INVESTIGATION

By the next visit to the castle, Paul and Stephen had met and having already carried out an investigation they were starting to form a good working relationship. On this second investigation of Kielder, to make things a little different, staff from the Castle was invited to join the rest of the team. There were two reasons for this: Firstly, having two independent participants might help to prove that previous events were not down to as Stephen put it "us all being mad" and secondly, the staff having more knowledge of the Castle could probably ask questions that are more definitive, it was hoped that would lead to answers which could be researched later. Two female staff members had elected to join us but choose to stay in a downstairs room doing some office work. If any of the spirits from the first visit decided to come through again they would join us if and when.

When the team arrived, Stephen asked Paul almost as soon as he got out of the car if he sensed anything. As Paul had not yet opened up, (opened up and tuned in to the spirit world), all he would say is that a particular window at the top of the castle drew him. Nothing further was said to ensure Paul had no prior knowledge of the location though Stephen did say that they would be able to visit that room later. The castle had not yet closed for the day so Paul and Stephen had a wander around the rooms, as Paul had never visited the location before it was useful to allow him to become familiar with the layout for later when the lights were out. Once the castle was closed for the day and all the visitors had left the team moved in and set up a base in a second floor room. The whole team split into three groups and set off for pre agreed locations to begin the investigation. The investigations started for Paul and Stephen when they first visited some out buildings. Paul came across the spirit person of what could be best described as a "street urchin looking young boy." This energy was quite shy and was simply peeping out from behind a doorway until Paul persuaded him to venture out. Once the young boy had, he spent the entire time whilst communicating with Paul holding Pauls right hand in a rather shy way. He told Paul that he had been a stable boy that had died in an accident, nothing sinister just an accident because of working in the stables. Now he came back to visit for no other reason than to be nosey. He did however tell Paul that there was a man who also returned to this area whom the boy was afraid of. He was so afraid of the man that he would not even discuss this man other than to say he also used to work in the same stables.

Rather regretfully, time was passing and Paul and Stephen had to move on and once he had established that the boy needed no help Paul said his goodbyes and left. Paul and Stephen now met up with the second of the three groups and set off with them to do a walk around of the interior of the castle. During the walk around, Paul picked up on several things. The first was in an upper room on the second floor he encountered the energy of an elderly man with legs so ruined by gout he could no longer hunt. Nevertheless, he liked to sit in his chair and look out the window. He was also a man who liked to paw the servant girls who worked at the castle when he was alive. He was a man of authority and as Paul put it "of high birth," so possibly one of the dukes from Alnwick Castle though Paul could not confirm that.

Moving on the team ventured into the room that housed the window Paul had commented on upon his arrival. Paul sensed the energy of a young woman in this room. This woman would spend hours and days standing at that window staring out, looking for a love that never did come back to her and if it was possible for anyone to die of a broken heart this woman had. Stephen would only comment that this tied in with known history of the location. The other thing in that room that Paul did feel; was a constant feeling of stepping out into darkness, or falling off a tall building. To date that has not been understood.

Lastly, on this first walk around Paul commented that an area in a corridor close to where there is now a cinema he felt that although there was a window in a wall, there should also have been a door or entrance. Stephen again without revealing any more detail confirmed this. Later at the end of the night as the team were gathering to leave, Stephen took Paul to the outer wall of that corridor and in fact, there are still clear traces of the former entrance. There is the significance attached to that door and the haunting of the castle, which was to become clearer later in the night. The members of the other group had assembled in another room inside the castle and Paul, Stephen, and the rest of their group joined them. As the team were sitting in a semi circle discussing plans for the night Paul noticed the spirit of a young man that he described as "dressed like a footman," though he did later say he had no idea how a footman would dress. What immediately struck Paul was the manner of this man, he said, "he had arrogance about him and a malicious nature."

Given this Paul kept a close eye on him and it was not long before the man appeared to make his mind up and marched around the outside of the semi circle and stopped behind a young man who was a friend of Stephen. Paul watched the energy stoop down towards Stephens friend and before he had a chance to give warning the young man began to shake violently, seemingly having some sort of seizure or fit. Paul quickly strode around to behind the young man and after a bit of a mental struggle forced the young footman to step back from the young man's energy. As soon as this happened, the young lad stopped shaking and appeared to slowly come to and understand where he was. Still very dazed and confused he could recall nothing of the whole incident other than being aware of the shouts and screams from some of the other team members and wondering why that was happening. This unnerved some team members but the more experienced people were looking forward to the rest of the night. Oddly from this time, about 20.30 hours the night and building went quiet, nothing really to report, however, as midnight approached things started to happen.

Using the Ouija some of the team started and had managed to begin to communicate with the Dukes but the information coming from them was scattered and not really making any sense. It seemed they grew bored with trying to make these ghost hunters understand and their energies faded away. Then just as last time Emma came through.

This time the team tried to glean more information about her life at the castle when she was alive. She explained through a combination of passing info through Paul and via the board that she used to do quite a lot of the cooking; it was her job to collect water from the well located in the castles grounds. What was puzzling to the team at the time was that she told of a door she used but the team knew of no evidence of it; this was before Stephen told them of Paul's comments about the missing door in the corridor. A plaque on the well was also incorrect, Emma also said. It states the war she lost her loved one to was the Boer War. Apparently, her lover did travel to Africa but it was not in this war he lost his life, however, she chose not to enlarge on that topic. It was hard to get answers for personal questions from Emma; she really did not want to answer these questions. She did like to joke and have fun however, for a time the team actually told silly jokes to Emma who would move the glass to yes or no depending if she approved or not. Not often that "comedians" get heckled from beyond the grave.

As the team were talking to Emma, they all could hear two male voices having a discussion downstairs. As there were only the two girls working downstairs, they asked Emma if these were spirit voices. She told us it was two of the Dukes talking about playing a trick on the girls. Emma was aware of other spirits but rarely encountered them; she could not really explain how that could be. The team asked Emma if the girls were still working downstairs. She told they had stopped working and taken to their sleeping bags and had nodded off. Some of the team set off to warn the girls and they were both fast asleep in their sleeping bags, much to the team's surprise, as some were not convinced that Emma was real. The girls were awakened and when told of Emma and of the duke plans they joined the rest of the team back up in the main room. Once everyone was settled, the séance was restarted. Almost at once they again were in contact with Emma, Stephen asked her if there was any part of the Castle and its grounds, she did not like? The glass moved at once to yes. Stephen started to recite different parts of the Castle but the glass stayed resolutely still. One of the two staff members who were observing asked if this was because they were in the room. The glass immediately shot to YES. Stephen explained to Emma she was not going to upset anyone by anything she "said" and again started to name different parts of the Castle. This time was different, the glass was moving rapidly and when he named "The Maze," it moved to "YES." He glanced at the two members of staff and one explained that she was one of the staff who had helped design the Maze. The team had not known this but Emma obviously did and she had not wanted to upset the staff member.

Stephen, who appeared to have empathy with this energy named Emma, asked many other questions about the possibility of Emma showing herself to us. Emma said it was possible for her to do it but she was not very happy about having to do it for two reasons. The first was that she was worried if she did show herself it would terrify someone. The second was that Emma thought if she did show herself or give us too much information the team would not return. This signified a natural break in proceedings so the team took the chance to go over plans for the rest of the night as well as try to digest the events that had happened so far.

Upon restarting Paul, Stephen with another team member decided to go off for a walk around of one-half of the building. At Paul's suggestion the rest of the team formed a group, including the female members and went off to hold a vigil in the room that Paul had encountered the old duke that used to like to "paw" the servant girls, he felt there would be a bigger reaction to a female presence in the room than a males. Paul and the rest of the group after spending time uneventfully in parts of the castle ended up sitting in a corridor adjacent to the cinema. Paul was sitting on the floor his back to the cinema Stephen and the other team member were standing facing Paul, both with video cameras running " recording" events hoping to capture any activity. What happened next is best described in Paul's own words: "As I was sitting on the floor doing the usual calling out asking for signs of any spirit presence, but not really sensing anything in the room I became aware of a spirit energy charging towards me from behind, emerging from the corridor leading into the cinema. At that time I could not sense if it was a male or female energy, only an overwhelming sense of anger and energy. I started instinctively to stand ready to face this but I did not have time to sound a warning to Stephen and the other team member, my full attention was focused on preparing me to deal with this energy. The best way I could describe the feeling is to picture yourself facing a large angry person running headlong at you for no reason you know of but knowing it was not going to be a friendly encounter. As I braced myself, I heard on the periphery of my consciousness Stephen swear aloud and swing the camera towards me with the other team member following his lead. The energy hit me like a freight train and for several minutes, I could only struggle with all my might to hold the emotions of this energy from overwhelming me. My senses were almost blown. Slowly I got a handle on controlling this energy and communicating with it. It rapidly became apparent it was a male energy and a worker connected with the castle. The only thing he would show me when I questioned him further was images of him working outdoors in the grounds of the castle, he would not tell me more as he was not interested in that topic. What did interest him and the topic he wanted to talk about, was why he was afraid to cross over to the other side. He was afraid that he would be sent to what he thought of as hell, or purgatory. When I questioned him why he felt this he would only keep telling me that he had "hurt the wife," he would not give any more details. I felt that he was ashamed for some reason and avoiding the topic. What also became apparent was that the initial surge of energy and anger was all a front. He was so afraid that I was there to make him cross to the other side he had decided that attack was the better form of defence.

Over what felt like many minutes, but in fact turned out to be only a short time, I learned in fact he felt incredibly alone, afraid and did want help. This sort of work helping spirit energies is an element of mediumship that many people are not aware of but one I had carried out many times before. I gradually convinced him that if he crossed he would not be sent "to hell."

Finally, he agreed to let me help him so I opened a link to the other side and as I did so I saw lit from the brilliant white light of the other side his wife and mother step forward to greet him. There was no hostility or anger coming from them, just a warm feeling of love and caring. His wife held out her hand to him and almost like a shy schoolboy on his first date he took it and both headed back towards the light of the other side joined by his mother. The last I saw of them as the light faded and the connection to the other side closed he was placing his head on her shoulder and they merged into a single soul.

I slowly gathered myself and opened my eyes, which I now realised I had had tightly shut. I found Stephen and the other team member staring with shocked looks on their faces. They told me that as I had stood they watched as a huge black cloud flew out the corridor and enveloped me in a circle from head to foot. After that all they could see was a shimmering cloud around me while I appeared to be talking to myself.

After several moments of excited babble, Stephen suddenly shouted, "I got it," meaning that he had just recalled the camera in his hand and that it had been pointing at me the whole time, including when the black shadow engulfed me. Stephen excitedly called on the radio and told the other group to meet us at the base room. Once we were all gathered, Stephen gave a brief recap on what had happened and that we had a video of it. We all gathered around the small screen of the camera jostling for the best position and Stephen pressed play. We all then saw "NOTHING." I can give you three guesses to who had not pressed "record." It maybe by the time I myself die and cross to the other side that I will forgive him and let him forget but I have not yet decided if he deserves that. Until then he will get reminded of it every time I tell this story and if you meet him, could you do the same please?"

THE LAST VISITS

The last two visits Stephen made in 2008 proved to be just as exciting. On his final visit, his best friend Gary Dixon decided to join him at Kielder Castle. He was a non-believer in the paranormal and had no problem with spending the night in the Castle. They were in part of the Castle that was thought to be the old stables, Paul and Stephen visited this area previously.

Nothing much had happened then but Paul if you recall had picked up on the energy of a small boy. There was a big table in the room so they decided to try table tipping, which is another method of trying to make contact with spirit. This is done by placing hands on top of a table and as you call out the table hopefully starts to move. Stephen was never a great fan of this but it was decided to try it and it took a while but eventually the table started to move. It was not possible to establish who the spirit was but by this point the table was starting to move quite violently. Just as Stephen was asking for more responses from the table his best friend suddenly removed his hands from the table and jumped back. He demanded that they stop straight away and refused to place his hands back on the table. After a little bit of discussion, it was decided to end the session and return to the base room. Back in the safety of the main room with the light on he explained to the rest of group what had happened. In the total darkness of the room, he had thought it was Stephen lifting the table in an attempt to frighten him. To try to catch him out he put his full weight on top of the table. At this point, he was lifted off the floor. Realising it was not possible to have lifted his weight from the opposite side of the table he wanted nothing more to do with it. Try as they may to give reassurances, the team could not persuade him to leave what he felt was the safety of the main room. Nearing the end of the night, two of the team decided they would go it alone in the attic. Just as they were about to go up the stairs to the attic something was dragged across the ceiling (the floor of the attic). Whatever was being dragged was then dropped. Despite this, they gingerly made their way up the stairs. About three quarters of the way up the stairs there was a huge bang behind the door to the attic. They did not know if this was a warning not to enter but if so it had the desired effect. They turned tail and headed back to the comfort of the main room.

Kielder Castle may not have the most ghost stories or be full of recorded history but it is safe to say it is at this location by far that Paul, Stephen and the other team members have experienced the most activity. Even today, they get chills down their spines every time they watch old video footage from their investigations at Kielder or get together to recall visits there. Paul still states to this day that the encounter with the energy in the corridor is also his scariest moment of his mediumship career, even though it had a successful conclusion.

From his visits, Stephen has collected many strange photographs. One is of a block in a wall, which appears to show the head and shoulders of a girl. When looking at this block normally through the day it does not look the same as the picture. The other picture is from the front of the Castle at night. In the mist there appears to be the shape of a person on horseback. You can see these pictures in this book and make your own minds up on what they appear to be.

On the other hand, you could always go visit the castle yourself, at night if you dare.

THE GHOST OF EMMA

When Paul and I were structuring the book we thought it would be best to dedicate a chapter to the Ghost of Emma. So much has happened between Emma and me that it would not be right to include the accounts within the main Kielder Castle chapter. A lot of people will read this chapter and probably think some of the accounts are farfetched or untrue. Not that I have to prove any of the accounts, although there are witnesses to do this, all I can do is tell them as they happened.

It is hard to think when my love affair with Kielder Castle and the Ghost of Emma all started. I remember in early 2004 I was spending most of my time online, researching new locations. To be honest at this time, this was my life and wouldn't stop until I had found new locations to visit. By chance I stumbled across Kielder Castle. I was aware of Kielder Reservoir but had no idea there was a castle tucked away near Kielder Village. The castle was run by the Forestry Commission and I noted from scouring their website that there was a story related to the ghost of a girl called Emma. There is a plaque on the well that tells what is supposed to be the story of the ghost. It is reported that the ghost was that of a maid called Emma who died from a broken heart waiting for her lover to return from the Boer War.

This was not a lot to go on but for some reason seemed spurred on to get in touch and see what the possibility would be to spend the night at the castle. To my total surprise I was invited to spend the night along with some of my friends. Unknown to me was that this was to be the start of an unbelievable journey.

The first contact we made with Emma was via an Ouija Board. Some of the questioning gave some quite remarkable answers and the physical experiences we were witness to were at times almost unbelievable. We quickly established that she was very active at the castle. One of the first things she told us was that she could see the Castle as it used to be and as it is now. She could see our electrical equipment on the table but did not know what it was because the items were not invented when she was alive. She was aware of other spirits within the castle but admitted for whatever reasons some of them ignored each other. Emma also liked to play tricks when she was alive but was not keen to play tricks on us. She liked jokes so we would tell her jokes and she would let us know by moving the glass if she thought the joke was funny or not.

On asking we could hear her whistle in the adjoining room and hear the sound of her feet running up the stairs. She could make lights flash and changed the temperature in the room to let us know when she was around us at the table. We asked many times if she would show herself but did not want to in case she frightened anyone so much that they did not want to return. We tried an experiment where we sent two people to a different room at the opposite side of the castle. We got one to ask the other five questions that would have a yes or no answer. Whilst these questions were ongoing we asked Emma to tell us the answers that were given by moving the glass. When the two people returned the five answers matched exactly the same to what Emma had told us.

From the very start Emma made it clear in the nicest way possible that she only wanted certain people on the glass when asking questions on the Ouija Board. Maybe this was to do with trust but I am not sure. It was also starting to become evident that she was asking me to go places alone in the castle. She would then answer questions to the others about me whilst I was in a different room. We must have visited Kielder Castle about two to three times each year in the early years and each year the activity and the effects of the place got more and more each visit.

On a separate visit, whilst on the Ouija Board, we were pushing for information about her surname and the story surrounding her at the Castle. She told us she had been a cook/servant and had, as the plaque on the well stated, made

129

many journeys to the well. She even admitted that she was aware people may have seen her spirit walking to and from that area. According to Emma the story on the well is not completely correct. She did die of a broken heart but her lover was not in the Boer War although he did go to Africa. She even gave information saying she married in Alnwick, Northumberland in a church with a strange looking tree. All of the time though I could not get the crucial bits of information I needed, such as her surname or the name of the church. I spent weeks on end researching but could not get any closer to unravelling the picture. In her defence she believed that once I knew everything about her that I would not return to the castle. I was aware from questioning that she liked the book Romeo and Juliet. On one visit I brought a copy of the book with me. I placed this in her room in the attic with some scribbled drawings I made on paper during an earlier visit. The book is there today and she has stated she would not be happy with anyone removing the book from the room. On the same visit I brought the book there was some odd things happened whilst conducting an Ouija board session. Emma said that she was going to put her hand through my hand. This hand was the one with my finger on the glass. This was possibly the coldest I have ever been and was shaking quite badly. At this time she pointed out that she wanted me to sit in the adjoining room alone. This normally happened so I set off into the room next door and sat on the steps. As the group questioned Emma I caught a glimpse of two of the ceilings lights going on for a split second. I was starting to shake, not with fright, but with the cold. My whole body was shaking and I started to switch off from the group. I then heard them shouting that Emma was sitting across my legs with her face pressed up against mine. The shaking and cold was quite unbearable and I think she realised that I was struggling and took her presence off me. The next day when I got home my face was burned with the cold. I can't believe for one minute that this was her intention but maybe she was just trying to prove her existence.

One thing that came from the Ouija Board sessions was the way in which Emma answered questions. It wasn't a simple yes or no it was a yes, yes or a no, no. Basically she would go to yes, back to the middle, then back to yes again. When she didn't know how to answer she took the glass to the middle. There are other spirits at Kielder and when they wanted to come through she would stop answering questions and move the glass in a circle. I believe this was her way of protecting us so we knew who we were dealing with. Emma has joined Ouija Board sessions at other locations where I have been to. Normally this has been to warn me of negative or bad spirits. This was not unexpected as Emma always said she would look out for me when I was conducting paranormal nights at other locations.

One location was at Castle Keep. She tried to warn me about the spirit of Charles and the spirits of the witches. This also happened at Tibbie Shiels Inn near Selkirk and at the Bebside Inn. Whilst on an Ouija board session a dark hooded figure walked across a doorway on the other side of a glass door. Nearly instantaneously the glass moved in the way Emma moved it. She said the dark figure was a warning to stop using the Ouija board.

I have also had some great information from mediums regarding Emma. Some of the information I am still trying to get my head around to this day. One medium that knew nothing of the stories surrounding Emma and myself stated that she had been with me before I had contacted Kielder and was pushing me in my thoughts to contact the location. The same medium stated that Emma and I stretched back to Egyptian times where we were together as partners but not married. What was even more mind boggling was that Emma confirmed this to be true. I remember on one of Paul's first visits whilst in the attic there were about seven of us (five girls plus Paul and myself). Emma let Paul know she was not happy with all the girls being in the same room with me.

Each time I visit Kielder as part of a group I am normally the first person there and as a rule the only one there until the rest of the group turn up. When all the staff has gone I open the front door and say: "Hi Emma I'm home." Do not know why I do this but always feel the need to do it. From here I normally just go upstairs and sit and read by myself. I can sit for hours alone hearing noises in different rooms but never feel scared or frightened. Some people think it is mad to be there alone but I feel so relaxed. I am sure over the coming years there will more accounts of activity between Emma and myself. Whilst writing this short chapter the hairs on the back of my neck have been standing on end. I may never get all the answers to my questions on Emma but it is safe to say Kielder Castle and Emma will always have a place in my heart.

The old lady who haunts the Bebside Inn

The Bebside Inn

Borthwick Castle

Brougham Hall

Castle Keep

The Ghost of Emma

High Head Castle

Kielder Castle - Ghostly image on the wall

Kielder Castle in the dead of night - note the ghostly mist.

Stephen (left) and Paul (Right)

North East Air Museum

Feeling the ghostly vibrations

North East Air Museum

The Schooner Inn

The Wallaw Cinema

Stephen and Paul

BROUGHAM HALL

PART 1

Brougham Hall lies two miles south of Penrith in the County of Cumbria. Situated near the River Earmont it is some 437 ft. above sea level. The Hall had a natural defensive position on the brow of a hill and had its own water supply in the form of a well in the courtyard. In A.D. 76 the Roman army arrived and built roads to the east of which is now Penrith. One of the roads, High Street, more than likely ran through the area of the Hall. The name Brougham is thought to come from two Old English words, the first word 'bru' meaning brow of a hill and the second word 'ham' meaning homestead. Putting these together produced the Old English word 'Burh-ham' which meant homestead near the fortification.

The first known owners were the de Burgham lords. The first of this family to be recorded is Wilfred de Burgham (1100-35). The family was able to keep their lands by what is known as drengage which was basically military service. The next probable owner was Odard de Burgham (1140-85) followed by his son Gilbert. Form Gilberts death in 1230 there is a gap in the history until 1272 at which point the de Broughams ran out of male heirs. As a result of this the estate was divided into three and split between Christiana de Burgham, William de Crackenthorpe and Henry Rydin. The hall was held in divided state until 1676.

The first Broughams of Brougham died out in 1609 but a branch of the family survived at nearby Scales. John Brougham bought the Hall in 1726 and his nephew, Henry Richmond Brougham, later built a mansion at High Head. Henry later inherited the estates and transformed Brougham into a mock-Gothic mansion. The 4th Lord Brougham sold the house in 1934 and partly being demolished it was used for a project in World War Two. It was taken over by the 35th Royal Tank Brigade. Brougham became one of the most secret British war projects: the Canal Defence Light tank. The 35th repaired many tanks and converted them into C.D.L tanks. They were fitted and tested with a 13-million candle powered strobe light fitted in their turrets. The idea was to confuse the enemy. A 'scatter' function created a terrible flicker effect as the light went on and off on the moving tanks turret. Most of the 35th Tank Brigade departed from Brougham in March-April 1944. The Tank was first used by British troops in the Normandy landings. After the War it was used in Africa and India and an improved form was adopted by the U.S. Army and called 'The Xenon Searchlight'.

After Polish refugees had been moved out the Hall lay unused. In 1948 a London Company bought it for £7,700. Then in 1967 it was purchased by a local builder in Penrith for £4,500. The involvement of Christopher Terry, a wealthy businessman, was to reverse the decline of Brougham Hall. After much time, money and effort Christopher managed to save Brougham Hall from extinction. There is an ongoing plan of restoration for the Hall which still carries on to this day.

To give you an overview of the Hall as it is today Christopher has kindly allowed me to use his Guide to Brougham Hall. The guide briefly describes the main features at the Hall. I will list these with a short description.

GUARD HOUE – built around 1550 the guardhouse stands at the main gate. The vaulted chamber serves as a reception centre and shop.

TUDOR BUILDING – dated 1480 to 1520 this is the oldest building, above ground level, identified so far. Originally a domestic building this was converted into stables by the Brougham Family

ARTESAN WELL- the 17 feet deep well has a natural water level above the Ice House, the cellars and the caverns nearby.

ICE HOUSE – dated 1843/44 the river water in winter was ducted into shallow pans in the meadows beneath the Hall and allowed to freeze. The frozen slabs were brought by cart to the Hall and placed in the Ice House together with provisions. It has a massive stone cavity wall and is very deep.

PELE TOWER – structure is dated C14th. It is one of the newest and smallest Pele towers in Westmorland.

SUNKEN GARDEN – After excavation it was decided to retain part of the exposed occupation level which appears to be divided into loose boxes and to date from the middle of the C16th.

THE MANSION – dates from the middle C16th. Substantially altered between 1787-1847 and included a magnificent armoury and a copy of the Bayeux Tapestry.

AIR RAID SHELTER – this is the latest phase of the building. Earlier was the base of the development of the CDL tank. The air raid shelters made use of the old wine cellars and were concreted over with a mound of earth some eight feet deep.

LORD CHANCELLORS DEN – the billiard room and the spiral staircase leading to the office was built in 1864 on the foundations of a much earlier tower.

ARBOUR – the feature designed by L.N. Cottingham enabled him to raise the West Terrace in 1843/4, when he added to the old domestic quarters and built a bridge across to the Cromwellian chapel on the other side of the re routed road. The road was bent by some thirty yards to accommodate the new wing. The road had previously passed much closer to the Pele Tower.

THE CHAPEL – was rebuilt in 1649 by Lady Anne Clifford on the site of a C14th chapel. From 1726 to 1934 it became Chapel to the Lords of Brougham.

WOODLAND WALK – built by an environmental youth scheme the walk starts at the Arbour, takes in a natural spring and views over the meadows.

CARRIAGE HOUSE – was built partly on the foundations of a massive medieval Hall.

In the meadows directly beneath Brougham was the scene of the Battle of Clifton Moor. This is reputed to be the last ever Battle on English soil. It took place between the forces of the British Hanoverian government and Jacobite rebels on the 19th December 1745. In the skirmish only twelve Jacobite rebels were killed, but the Government forces sustained a loss of about one hundred killed and wounded, including some officers. The only Jacobite officer wounded was the Macdonald of Glengarry chief. The only prisoner taken was a footman of the Duke of Cumberland. A skeleton wearing tartan, found in the 1920's near Stanhope, is believed to have been a Jacobite casualty of the skirmish.

There are various ghostly stories surrounding the Hall. One of the main stories is the Legend of Brougham. This Legend came about due to a skull that was found in one of the walls when restoration work was taking place. The skull has 3 puncture wounds in the top of it. Past owners are said to have removed the skull and from that time onwards the Hall suffered much torment. The skull is said to be that of an unnamed soldier who fought in the Crusades. A plaque has been erected which tells of the Brougham Legend. It reads, "Unknown soldier from a sunlit shore. Who paid the price in an unknown war. For an unknown God in an unknown time. Peace eternal now be thine. Pray lie within this ancient wall and guard that it shall never fall."

Ghostly shadows have been seen passing workshop

windows. When workers have gone outside to check there was nobody there. In an area next to the Mansion there is a stone table set on the ground. This table is supposed to be the scene of worship and even possible sacrifice. Ghostly figures have been seen in the area of the woodland walk. Sounds from the Battle of Clifton Moor are said to have been heard. The crashing of swords, screaming of soldiers and horses galloping are just some the noises.

Due to unforeseen circumstances I found myself travelling alone to Brougham Hall to spend the night. The excitement of spending the night on such a great location had made me forget the fact that I would be there totally alone. I arrived pretty early on site at Brougham and was quite surprised by the size of the place. The whole area of the Hall was bigger than I expected. It was a glorious day with the sun beaming down. My first fright of the day was not a ghostly one but the welcome you get when you go through the main gate. A sensor triggers when you walk through the main gate and sets off a welcome message. This gave me quite a fright and in my head hoped that the sensor was switched off during the night. The last thing I wanted was for it to go off in darkness, especially if I was nowhere near it.

I was met by Christopher Terry who took me around the Hall and told me about all the different history surrounding the Hall and what was happening in respect to the restoration. A great deal had been restored and so much so there were now businesses housed in parts of the Hall. It was a great setting on a great day. I had lots of time on my hands so started by having lunch in the grassed area of the Hall. I used this time to familiarise myself with all the different areas as I knew when the night fell I would not have the same luxury. I also managed to perfect the timer on my camera. Nobody else was with me so I got lots of photos in various parts of the Hall. I did get some strange looks of some people when they saw me running away then standing still looking into nowhere. Later in the afternoon Christopher took me to see High Head Castle. As we spent time there the night began to fall and by the time I arrived back at Brougham it was pitch black.

Armed with my night vision camera, torch and digital camera I sat myself in a little alcove built into the wall. Sitting here it began to dawn on me that maybe it wasn't the best idea to be alone. Not just for the fear element but more for the safety side of things. If something had of happened then I would have been there until Christopher turned up in the morning. As I sat alone the natural light of the moon gave the Hall a very eerie feeling. Add the bats into the equation and my heart was beginning to pump. It is hard to explain but I always thought it would be very hard to talk to the camera whilst filming. If anything it was easy but I think the main reason for talking is that it takes away the fear. After some time I decided to get up from the relative safety of the alcove and start my tour of the Hall.

In these situations the senses are heightened to the limit. I could have heard a pin drop over the other side of the Hall. I made my way up to an area above the main gate where there is a small spiral staircase. I sat myself on the staircase and started to ask out to see if there were any spirits present. All the time I was keeping my fingers crossed that the sensor had been switched off below me. After some time with no responses I decided to move on. To exit this area you have to walk down a steep slope of grass. I had just told myself to take care as the grass was damp, when my feet went from under me. My equipment went backwards as I slid down the hill. I don't know why but I just started laughing. Surviving the fall I headed for an area of the Lord Chancellors Den where there is a statue of Christ on the cross. This statue is now laid downwards with Christ looking towards the sky. Various mediums have picked up the presence of a girl kneeling at the foot of the cross so I reluctantly positioned myself in this area. Again I sat quiet for a while then started asking to see if there were any spirits present or if the spirit of the girl was present. There were a few cracks in response to some of my questioning but nothing you couldn't rule out for something natural. Next I moved to the area where the skull is positioned in the wall. Again with little or no response I decided it was time for a break before I continued. I think the break was more to try and help my mind decide if I wanted to continue. I knew which two areas were left to investigate and was not looking forward to it one little bit.

After I had rationalised everything I decided to make my way to the start of the woodland walk. All sorts of things were running through my head at this point. Ghostly figures and the sounds of the Battle of Clifton that had been heard by various people were right there in my head. Not to mention any crazy human like myself who likes to take midnight walks in the woods. I gingerly made my way down towards the arbour where the path turns left down through the woods towards the meadows, the meadows being the scene of the Battle of Clifton. I decided to leave the investigation of the Arbour for when I returned from the Woodland Walk. This return was not going to be long. I managed to walk about 100 metres when I am positive I caught site of two figures in the woods. Whatever I had seen was gone within the blink of an eye. That was enough so I headed back to towards the relative safety of the Arbour. It was so quiet I could hear my heart beating and it was beating very fast. The Arbour is basically a row of stone pillars holding up the land above it. I positioned myself at the far end so I could get a view along the row of columns and a view of the woods. Not that I could see anything but it made me feel a bit safer. I plucked the courage up to start asking out. Each time I asked out I would cringe in anticipation of the possible response. Just when I thought all was going ok there were two cracks in response to one of my questions. The crack sounded like a bit of wood being stood on then breaking. Again my eyes caught movement in the woods so I decided to retreat back up to the Hall. I got about half way when I remembered I had taken my hat off in the Arbour and had forgotten to pick it up whilst making my hasty retreat. I am not afraid to say it but I ran into the Arbour, grabbed it and ran back up to my car that was parked at the Hall.

Trying to make sense of things whilst sitting in the car I remembered there was one last place I had to go to. The final location at Brougham for me to investigate was The Chapel. As with the woods I was not looking forward to this at all. I could not get access to the Chapel itself but could still walk in the graveyard. To access the Chapel there is a small bridge across the road that runs along the side of the Hall. Once inside my torchlight was catching the eyes of rabbits that were out in force throughout the graveyard. I edged slowly over a grassed area towards the Chapel. I have no idea why but had the sense there was the spirit of a young girl in the area of the Chapel. I got to one end of the Chapel and sat myself up against the wall. Praying in a church is normal but I was praying for something different. There were many trees and each gave the impression of someone looking out around the corners to see what I was doing. By this point I was going out of my mind. One part of my head was saying calm down and the other was telling me I am sitting in a graveyard. I have no idea how but I plucked up the courage to start asking out. All was quiet for about ten minutes until I heard what sounded like a whistle or the beginning of someone singing. I tried to stay to ask out more but my head was totally gone. I couldn't last anymore. I was a paranoid wreck. I made my way back to the car for a final time and decided to head for home.

My stay alone at Brougham Hall is the single scariest thing I have experienced at any location. Not because of ghostly activity, of which I believe there was some, but for the full range of emotions I put myself through. The fear at times mixed with the mind games was unbearable and something I would not wish on anyone. Watching my video footage back makes for excellent viewing and has given me some ideas for TV in the future.

BROUGHAM HALL

PART 2

HALLOWEEN INVESTIGATION

On the lead up to the investigation at Brougham Hall Paul, having read some parts of Stephen solo vigil was eager to do a full night there. Before that happened however Paul, Stephen and James who is, a friend of Stephen and a photographer visited the hall a few weeks prior to the investigation to do a photo shoot. While the main business of the day was to get some good shots for publicity prior to the event and for this book, Paul was also keen to get a taste for what energies were around. Arriving early, the first order of business was breakfast at the excellent on site café. 30 minutes later with a good breakfast and an excellent cup of coffee inside them Christopher Terry, the owner of the hall had arrived. After introductions had been made it was agreed that as Christopher had a busy schedule that day Paul and Stephen would get on with the shoot and meet up with Christopher later.

The photo shoot itself would take about 90 minutes and Paul had the chance to visit most of the site. Some areas interested him more than others of course but he did feel in one area in particular very uneasy, but more of that later. Nevertheless, one area that neither he, nor the groups attending on the investigation night had a chance to gain access to was the Tudor Building at the entrance to the main courtyard.

Here as he was posing with Stephen for pictures he could sense they were being watched. After the pictures were completed for that area and Stephen was off getting some solo shots done Paul took the chance to have a "psychic" look around.

What he found was in the top of the Tudor building there is a window; in there Paul could sense and just see due to the acute angle of vision a spirit woman looking down. Despite Paul's best attempts to draw this woman into communication, she simply stood and stared down at him. Paul knew that she could hear and see him but while curious, she had no desire to chat. After several attempts, Paul gave up and joined Stephen and James. The shoot completed they met up with Christopher in a courtyard adjunct to the café and Christopher asked Paul if he could pick up things in daylight?

When Paul confirmed he could he was asked if there was anything in the area he picked up on. Paul immediately pointed to an area of blank wall between the Icehouse and a pottery workshop; he said he "was not happy with that area for some reason". As the area was simply an area of blank stonewall his puzzlement was understandable. However, no comment was made and the group continued on to view the Icehouse. During the actual investigation the reason for Pauls disquiet at that area of wall will be made clearer.

As a result of a conversation with Christopher, the group was given permission to visit another property that Christopher owned; this was about a 30-minute drive from the hall. There will be more on this location though in another chapter sadly we cannot reveal its name or location as it is the site of a private home. Sufficient to say Paul as he entered the property stopped dead and revealed that he had literally walked into a "wall of energy," something that was a first for him.

On the lead up to the Brougham hall investigation, which was to be carried out on Halloween 2010 there was lots of interest from both the public and the press, therefore, when the night came around the event was fully booked with a full house of twenty people. While it may have been possible to add more people to that number and in fact, Paul had to introduce a

149

reserve list so great was the interest, it was felt that this number would allow people to have the best experience of the hall.

Too many people and they would have been on top of each other. Stephen was the first to arrive on site to be greeted by Christopher, Paul arrived some thirty minutes later and the first thing he did was step out the car and trip on a large boulder. No real damage except to his ego but a bang on the knee meant he suffered the rest of the night. However, it did remind Paul and Stephen that they should heed the advice they always give to groups before the start of every event on safety and the use of torches when needed.

After another walk around the whole site prior to the guests arriving both Paul and Stephen were ready for the night. Once the guests had all arrived and been greeted with a warming drink the night began. After a safety briefing by Paul and Stephen followed by a walk around the site to allow all the guests to familiarise themselves with the layout, the group split into two. One of the groups led by Paul headed for an area of the site known as The Bunker. This area is not as a rule open to the public and many day visitors would have walked by the entrance or over the top of the bunker without knowing it was there. Extreme Ghost Hunting had been given exclusive access to it by the owner Christopher. However to gain entry the groups had to descend a temporary metal ladder. Paul later commented that climbing down the ladder guided only by torchlight was a scary start for some of the guests.

Once all were safely down the ladder Paul led them to the back of the bunker where a table and chairs had been set up. Paul suggested that some of the group would like to do some table tipping and the rest could keep an eye out for any visual anomalies. There was no shortage of volunteers to try the first table tipping session. Under Paul's guidance, the volunteers positioned themselves around the table and began asking for sign of any spirit presence to move the table. Within a short time they reported that the table was vibrating. As this was happening, Paul began to be aware of the presence of two-spirit men. Both were wearing what looked to be WW2 uniforms. One was quite young and shy the other was older and obviously in authority.

As both Paul and the group asked questions of the two men, the table began to react with greater urgency. With guests feeling the table angling away and towards them at steeper and steeper angles plus at times appearing to lift off and bounce over the floor. The older of the two spirit men was the one who took the lead. He had been in charge of a group that had used the shelter to both work in and at times take refuge. Paul was shown pictures by spirit of large groups of men and women gathering with mugs of tea and thick sandwiches being handed out.

During the session an odd thing occurred. Some guests insisted that they could see an odd glow that was hovering near the table and at times moving around. This quite excited some until Paul noticed that in fact the luminous face of his watch was the culprit. However, it was odd that Paul having owned this watch for many years and worn it on many occasions for investigations had never seen the face glow in such a manner.

The younger of the two men as stated previously was quite shy and Paul was keen to draw information from him. The man seemed quite nervous of speaking in front of the older man who was senior in rank. With some persuasion, he started to give some information. The main emotion that he passed to Paul was of abject misery. He came over as a sensitive man who hated the male dominated atmosphere at the site. He in particular felt animosity towards the older man who it appeared had bullied him verbally, teasing him for his unmilitary manner and attitude. All this young man wanted to do was to return to his home and way of life, it was obvious that he was a conscripted man unprepared for military life. It was during these exchanges that at time the table in response to question from the group was at its most active. Which Paul felt given the shy nature of the young man was odd. As the young man got his tale

151

off his chest and his presence faded the tables activities slowed. Later when guests from the other group visited this area, some of which were mediums and sensitives, they were given the names Samuel and Maxwell.

Paul's group next agreed to spend some time in a smaller room at the entrance to the bunker. In here, most of the group expressed feeling apprehensive but could not explain why; they simply had a desire to leave the room and the area as soon as possible. Later when the other group visited this area, they reported that some could smell and "taste" the stench of blood in the room. As if, a bloodbath had occurred at some time. Later in the night after both groups had visited the area a trigger object, a coin surrounded by powder to detect any movement was left on the table. At the end of the night, the area was revisited but there appeared not to have been any movement, which giving the level of activity on the night was slightly disappointing.

The format of the first half of the night was to have the two groups swap locations, therefore, Paul and his group made their way to the cellars. Once again, this is an area of the hall that is not open to the public. Access this time was a little easier then getting into the bunker; simply having to negotiate stone steps. The layout at the bottom was of a series of small rooms leading off from a corridor that led on to an area that was open to the elements. From that open area two larger rooms led off under the terrace garden. Many of the rooms were empty, some were filled with what looked like general rubble from the ongoing refurbishment but one had old household items stored. Items that included a child's rocking chair, a table and some garden tools. In the corridor, some chairs had been placed to allow some of the group to sit. As the group entered the area and settled down Paul was aware of a spirit man standing near the room with the rocking chair in. Later another group who visited the area on the night felt that this man's name was Gregory.

Paul saw that the man was dressed in tight breeches,

short boots with a dirty shirt and jacket. As the man was rather portly, it was not a fetching outfit. What was more annoying to Paul was the man's attitude and the sneer fixed on his face as he observed the group. He appeared to have a very arrogant attitude and most definitely considered himself a cut above anyone in the group, especially the women of whom he seemed to hold a particular resentment. Though Paul did say this, he felt it was more to do with the general attitude of men to women as inferior beings that would have prevailed during the time that this man lived.

As the group were settled they began to ask out for signs of any spirit activity, until then Paul had not told anyone of the man's presence, people in the group began to complain of feeling "odd" and "uncomfortable". One member described it as though she was being stared at. Which of course Paul knew was exactly what was happening. After asking if everyone was happy Paul asked for all the torches to be turned off. The area in the corridor became very dark though there was natural light spilling in from the open area at the end. As eyes adjusted to the gloom people reported seeing and hearing the spirit of a little girl at the end of the corridor near the entry steps. Many also reported seeing a dog. One woman commented that she felt her hair being tickled or ruffled. Just as she was saying this there came from the other end of the corridor one of the most blood curdling screams Paul had ever heard. Though startled he did also say he was also quite cheered that activity had occurred that was enough to cause such a scream. Of course following the scream there was a great deal of confusion with torches being turned on, people heading for the exit without really caring what the reason for the scream was and others seemingly rooted to the spot.

After a few minutes, Paul restored order and found that there were still about six people of the group remaining. Then a high-pitched squeak gave him a clue to what could have been the cause of the scream. Shining his torch beam towards the squeak he found a very confused and annoyed sounding bat flying around, no doubt wondering why his roost had been disturbed. Once this had been communicated to the rest of the group most of them returned but some opted to head to the base room that was only a short distance away.

Order restored the remainder of the group again settled and began asking for signs of spirit activity. Paul had noticed that the man, Gregory had disappeared but the young girl was still there. She was running up and down the corridor where some of the group were sitting and seemed much happier now that Gregory was gone. Paul's attempts to communicate with her only resulted in her stopping her running up and down and waving shyly at him. Apart from that, she appeared to have no interest in making a noise, or showing herself.

To try to see if there was any other spirit people present that he could not sense and maybe to encourage Gregory to return, Paul suggested a séance using the table in one of the smaller rooms. The séance was quickly set up, and due to space being limited; only four people were able to gather around the table. Attempts to get any response went on for about 15 minutes but apart from some very loud thuds coming from the stairs, it sounded as if a sack of potatoes had been thrown down, and dare it be said a body, nothing else happened.

Due to the lack of any further activity and the cold starting to penetrate it was agreed to head back to the base room. After almost everyone had left, Paul and another member of the group were having a last look around and getting some pictures of the bat that now appeared to have gone to roost. By chance they both shone their torches into the room with the child's rocking chair. As they did they saw the chair starting to slowly rock. They both watched it for a little while to see if it would stop; maybe it was moving as a result of being accidentally nudged as others in the group left, however, it kept moving at a constant pace until the man with Paul asked out "Who is moving the chair?" At once, it stopped dead despite their attempts to make it move again in the same manner by nudging it or looking for a draught as the cause they could not replicate the movement. Who moved the chair and why is it as yet unexplained?

As the time was drawing near it was agreed for all groups to take a midnight break and they headed back to the base room. Once everyone was in there and everyone had a hot drink in their hands people were comparing experiences. It was found that even for differing groups visiting locations at differing times the information and occurrences were remarkably similar. The old wartime bunker was one example in that the way the table moved and the information on the two men who appeared to both groups was the same.

After everyone was refreshed, Stephen and Paul introduced the second half of the night. They take pride that they structure the night in a different way to other groups. Instead of having a rigid approach to when and where guests can go Paul and Stephen offer them the chance to go off to a location of their choice alone or in smaller groups. Always off course with a radio for safety, and strict understanding of being respectful of the location. They also offer people the opportunity to carry out solo vigils that they can record via a hand held night vision video camera. Any volunteers can choose their own location for such a vigil or a location suggested by Paul or Stephen based on historical knowledge and or psychic intuition. There was only one volunteer to carry out a solo vigil, a friend of Stephens who wanted to spend some time in the Icehouse. The rest agreed they wanted to head to a ruined part of the hall that is located on the vehicular access road that leads into the hall. This is known as the Lord Chancellors den. Inside the ruin is a huge cross laid flat with the figure of Jesus upon it with ropes around hands and feet. Once again, with safety being paramount, Paul warned that within the ruins and on the entry point there are some deep holes. However, most of the group wanted to head into the building. While they were inside exploring Paul stayed outside with the others. As he was tuning into his surroundings he was presented with mental images of

155

Winston Churchill and an image of a tank battle. This being totally at odds with his surrounding Paul really did not know what to make of this but stored it away to mention later. Any of you who read the previous chapter Stephen's history of the castle will know that in fact, Churchill did visit the site and there is a tank connection, although at the time Paul was unaware of this. Inside the ruins, some of the group appeared to be picking up random bits of information but nothing specific. Some of the information was names such as Archibald Singer and Old London Town as well as a feeling of "Chemistry", to date however there is no connection that can be made with that information. Leaving the ruins of the Lord Chancellors Den behind them the group decided to venture out along a route that took in the top half of the woodland walk and terrace then would be ending at the Arbour. As part of that route, they had to pass an area that is easy to pass unnoticed. It is a small recess in the wall of the building known as The Mansion. Paul was particularly keen to see if any of the group would feel or pick up on anything in that area. On his and Stephens walk around on the day of the photo shoot Paul felt very uncomfortable in that area, with feelings of apprehension and evil deeds, however, he did not share these details wanting the groups to go in "cold" so to speak. He stood back to observe the group's reactions. At once, several members complained of feeling uneasy, though none to the same degree as Paul who had to force himself to go near the place. As some of the other mediums in the group focused on the area the information Paul had picked up was confirmed by them. Along with the feeling of unease that many felt there were also feelings that several others had attacked one man. They had stabbed at and cut the lone mans throat. Some complained of smelling blood and one guest had the same sensation as Paul felt, the feeling and taste of blood in the mouth. Not pleasant and both Paul and the group were happy to leave the area and move on.

They headed down some slippery stone steps, where care was needed headed along a path towards the Arbour.

Again, Paul kept quiet about most of the information he had picked up on during his walk around except for one part. On that first walk around, he felt strongly that a wooden entrance gate or postern set into the wall leading into the grassy area from the road had some significance. He was constantly fed the term "Traitors gate" but the owner of the hall had said there was no other significance of the gate except as a convenient entry point from the road. Despite this Paul was still getting the same information just as strongly now. Only a few of the group who could pick up on anything about the gate, they were using such terms as "Devils Gate". There was also the feeling of the gate being used by women creeping in to the fields around the hall. To date there has been no historical confirmation of any of this information and if any reader has some we would be grateful if they would contact the authors.

The group then settled themselves in the Arbour where some plastic garden chairs had been provided for the night. As instructed by Paul they turned off torches and sat to allow their eyes to adjust to the light. Oddly, as they did the sight of the night sky glistening above them devoid of the light pollution that dulls the stars was a major talking point. The sky was alight with stars that would probably not have been visible if looking at the night sky from a town or city. Paul himself felt he would love to return on a warm summer night and simply spend hours lying in the field gazing at the sky.

The groups slowly turned their focus back to the business of the night and settled quietly to observe and listen to the surroundings. As they did many started to comment that they could see people in the woods to the left of them. Paul conscious of the brain's ability to play tricks in such an environment asked then them all to try looking away for a few minutes then back onto the same spot. The group did that but as they refocused their eyes in the same area, they again told of seeing shifting shadows within the trees. One guest also told of seeing the figure of a man, sword in hand on the pathway they had just came down. Most of the guests said they felt as though the area around the Arbour in the woods and field had been the site of much activity. They told of seeing people running around, horses being ridden and water being fetched to wash out blood from wounds and clothing. One guest reported seeing and hearing the rumble of "cartwheels" on the road next to the field and of soldiers marching towards the hall. Soldiers dressed in an old-fashioned style of uniform and with "ordinary" people marching behind the soldiers.

Within the Arbour itself, the overwhelming feeling the group picked up on was of "plotting" of secret meetings being held by men who by the style and quality of their clothing appeared to be in positions of power. They were plotting a pact that would topple or depose another man and making plans to get rid of this man. One guest did pick up on the date of 1842. Nevertheless, the entire group felt that this area was a much-used place for those that wanted to meet out of sight of the hall over the years. Not always for political or personal plans to be made for revenge but also for meeting of lovers. All agreed though for such a small area that it was a hugely interesting place.

The group decided to head back to the base room, it being a little chilly now in the early hours another hot drink seemed a good idea but it was agreed to take a circuitous route and visit the area around the chapel. With Paul leading the way the group headed back up the terrace steps, once again almost all the eyes were turned skywards marvelling at the display the heavens were putting on. Once the group arrived at the church however all eyes were focused forwards and a quiet air fell over the whole group. Paul was also feeling the disquiet that the rest of the group was noticing. In the trees to the rear of the chapel the whole group had the feeling of being watched. Not in an unpleasant way more with the sense of curiosity emanating from the energies in the trees peeking out. Paul's feeling was "as though the energies were almost not human." An odd description but Paul has learned to trust the information he receives. He did not voice his thoughts however, preferring to let the group come up with their own opinions. For about 10 minutes the whole group stayed stock still, their eyes were already well adjusted to darkness having been out doors for some time. So without the need for torchlight the group could see small shadows flitting between the trees and there was the distinct sound of branches being moved and leaves on the ground being trod through. Gradually the group started to discuss the impressions and emotions they were experiencing. It was agreed that the energies in the trees were afraid of the group but also curious. It was also agreed that they were of children. Most of the group confirmed Paul's initial feelings that the feeling was of feral, wild and untamed children.

None of the group could establish any communication with any of the children, though curious their natural fear of them as a group of adults seemed to hold them back. It was noted however that the females of the group seemed to be less threatening to the children than the males. After a further period the chill was growing due to being stood still, it was obvious that there was to be no communication with the children the group said their goodbyes and returned to the base room.

Over mugs of hot drinks Paul and Stephen consulted with the group on what they felt like doing for the rest of the event. Paul's prime suggestion was a séance in the sunken garden. There is a large slab of stone in that area and Paul had felt on his walk around before the guests arrived that there was a "reception committee" awaiting any group who wanted to visit there.

The group was quite keen on the idea though some merely wanted to observe rather than join in the séance. Upon arrival at the garden, a small group went into the sunken area where the stone slab was located and the rest grouped in the garden above. Paul preferred to observe the séance rather than take part so in one of the groups Helen, an experienced medium, agreed to lead the séance. As is the normal procedure prayers were first said and then the group joined hands and the séance began. Almost at once, a change in Helen became plain. As she began to speak her voice was of a frightened young girl. At first it was difficult to decipher what she was trying to say but as the minutes passed her voice became stronger, as though the spirit coming through her grew used to using her voice.

What became very plain is that this young girl had gone through a horrifying experience. Her name was Mary or Marie and at the time of her death aged around 12 or 13, she told that she had been sacrificed or "cut open" on that stone while still alive. Some of the guests taking part in the séance felt that there had almost been an autopsy carried out on her while she lived. However Paul felt it is more likely that this feeling was a result of the sacrifice. Helen also complained at this time of a considerable amount of pain in her head, as though a blow had been struck, maybe in order to finally stun this poor soul and put her out her misery.

This story and the emotions surrounding it powerfully affected the people taking part in the séance and it was agreed to close the circle of the séance but first Helen offered help to the spirit of the young girl. The whole group was asked to focus their energies on helping the young girl to find some peace and cross to the other side to get help if she wished to do so.

The group completed this and there was a break in activities to allow people to recover from the emotions of this séance. During the whole time this had being going on Paul had been keeping a close eye on the spirit figure of a man standing at the rear of the garden. He was dressed as a monk, in a hooded one-piece garment with a rough texture, but Paul felt his manner and attitude did not tie in with this attire. Instead he appeared to be very arrogant and rather contemptuous of the group séance and their concern for the young girl.

Once the group had recovered, Paul told of this man and suggested using the Ouija board to see if the group could make contact. A new group of people stepped in for this attempt; four people gathered around the board and placed their fingers on the planchette. The man in the garden was fully aware that the group was trying to communicate with him. Once again Paul could see he was quite contemptuous of this. In fact so irked was Paul by his attitude and waves of arrogance flowing from this man he did something that as a rule he would not. He decided to bait the man. As the group was asking out as they grouped around the board, Paul began to berate the man. Paul could see and the group could sense by the glass twitching, that he was starting to get a reaction. Each time Paul insulted or berated the spirit there was a reaction both on the face of the man and by the glass moving. Once in fact the man did take a step towards the group around the board but stopped and stepped back. Paul sensed that the man prided himself on his self-control and most defiantly held himself above what he considered the common herd.

Despite Paul's and the group's efforts there was no further reaction from the board and it was decided to close the séance down. Though Paul has vowed to himself that as far as he is concerned, the situation between him and the "monk" is not over and they will meet again. Back at the base room over the last hot drink of the night, plans for the last activity of the night were discussed.

In a small room just off the main courtyard, it was decided to hold another séance using the Ouija board. As this was the only area that was within the main part of the hall, there was interest to see if there would be any responses. To date most of the investigations and séance had taken place in locations on the fringes of the estate.

Paul and some others from the group remained in the base room for an informal Q&A while the rest went off to carry out the final séance of the night. Once the "séance" group had settled down and the observers were comfortable they began. At once, the planchette began to move and a tale was told of two guards that tied in with the emotions and sensations felt by many in the guardhouse, the area that Paul had described as a

161

"small niche." It appeared that the two men, named Mark and John, though it was felt that this may not be their real names were love rivals for a woman named Zenya. As a result, John plotted to kill Mark in the area of the estate already visited during the evening, The Arbour. John had made an earlier attempt to kill Mark by attacking him in the guardhouse and stabbing him in the throat. As already stated this was picked up as a throat being cut by the group when they visited that area. John felt that Mark was winning the battle to woo Zenya and this time was determined to finish the job. He enlisted the help of others but would not say whom or how he managed this. They lured Mark to the Arbour where he was killed. Even at this séance the brooding presence of Mark could be felt. John told most of this tale as it was claimed that Mark could not read or write while John could. Though Mark did attempt to spell out some words, it was not a great success.

So the account was one sided and as with all one-sided tales it must be viewed with a little suspicion. Lastly as the séance ended there came through the board the energy of a young boy aged about 7 years old. He could only say that his name began with an R. Some of the participants in the séance said "he had a cheeky grin" as they could see him in their minds eye. Sadly he told of having drowned because of falling into the well that sits in the courtyard. Today the well is protected by a stout metal grid but that would not have always been the case.

Time was now heading towards 3am and a fine rain was again falling. Many of the guests had a long drive ahead so it was decided that it was a good time to end the night. Brougham Hall it was felt by the group had much more to give and they had only scratched the surface. Many of the group had experienced faint and isolated images and sounds around the site. They had heard the sound of horse's hooves and the rumble of solid metal wheels on the road leading up to the castle. Another had a fleeting glimpse of a woman in a white dress with the name Arrabel or Annabel in an area near the Manor house. Many more had sensed a great battle taking place in the field adjacent to the road leading to the hall. So the Hall has more secrets that is has to give up. It seems that the spirits there like to play their cards close to their chest. Not revealing everything at once or in some cases simply wishing not to have this world know of the crimes committed. Only further investigation will tell.

Lastly, the reason why Paul felt so much disquiet at what appeared to be a solid stone wall when he first visited the hall. It seems that Christopher had revealed to Stephen and Stephen alone, that area is where the so-called "Cursed Skull" was sealed up. The tale told by Stephen in the history of the hall before his solo vigil. So that is at least one mystery the hall did agree to give the secret to.

The rest will have to wait…

NORTH EAST AIR MUSEUM

THE HISTORY

The Museum is set on the site of what once was RAF Usworth. As the name of the museum suggests it is located in the North East of England near to Sunderland. There is much history surrounding RAF Usworth and a great many thanks must go to the Museum who allowed me to use the history they have in place already.

The grass airfield opened in autumn 1916 at Hylton for use by the region's Home Defence unit (36 Squadron). It was built on (and also known as) West Town Moor and facilitated a detachment of various aircraft. In June 1917 the Squadron HQ moved in fully with the Bristol Fighter being the main aircraft type in operation. Detachments were also established at Ashington and Seaton Carew. By this time the airfield was also being referred to as Usworth. 36 Squadron only lasted until June 1919 before being disbanded, the airfield becoming disused.

The Airfield was re-acquired in 1930 with 607 Squadron of the Royal Auxiliary Air Force becoming established in March and remained here until October 1939 when the Squadron moved to Acklington. During this time a number of different aircraft were operated including the Wapiti, Demon and Gladiator. In early 1937 the number of airframes at the airfield was increased with the arrival of 103 Squadron from Andover with their Hinds. During the summer of 1938 the Squadron re-equipped with Fairy Battles, but a few months later had moved out to Abingdon.

During the early war years the airfield was developed to include two runways as well as a perimeter track. An attack on the airfield was planned by the Luftwaffe for August 15th 1940, but this was intercepted by fighters from Acklington, Catterick and Usworth before the bombers were anywhere near the field.

By this time 607 Squadron had returned equipped with Hurricanes for two short periods (June 1940-Sept 1940 and Dec 1940-Jan 1941). Fighter support was also provided briefly by 43 (September 1940-December 1940) and 64 (May 1940) Squadrons with Hurricanes and Spitfires respectively.

By early 1941 training had replaced the fighter role as the main activity with the arrival of 55 Operational Training Unit from Aston Down with over one hundred aircraft (Blenheim, Defiant and Hurricanes). The large number of aircraft means a satellite airfield had to be established at Ouston. The OTU moved out during April 1942 and the airfield returned to care and maintenance until the formation of 62 OTU in June with their Ansons. The unit remained at Usworth until July 1943 at which time it moved to Ouston, the proximity of the local balloon barrage at Sunderland being the reason used. For the remainder of the war the airfield was very quiet with little activity.

The end of the war (and removal of the balloon barrage) saw the arrival of 23 Reserve Flying School in February 1949 who operated a number of different trainer types until disbanding in July 1953. Between the years 1951-1953 2 Basic Air Navigation School was also based there with their AvRoe Ansons. Other users of Usworth during this period were the Durham University Air Squadron with their Chipmunks (May 1949-Oct 1957), 664 Squadron with their Austers (Feb 1954-Mar 1957) and a number of gliding schools.

On 3 July 1962, the airfield was purchased by Sunderland Corporation for £27,000 and reopened as Sunderland Airport. Sunderland Corporation re-laid the runways and renovated the hangar, and in June 1963 Sunderland Flying Club came into being. The following year an Open Day and commemorative ceremony took place on June 28 1964 to celebrate the rebirth of what was now Sunderland Airport.

There was a modest flying display and pleasure flights were made available in a visiting Dakota. The cost of such flights was 15 shillings for adults and 10 shillings for children, the Dakota being kept busy all day. However, its short runways precluded any use on a regular basis by other than light twins.

The appearance of a Dakota in 1964 was a result of a brave attempt by Newcastle based Tyne Tees Airways to operate a charter airline from Sunderland. Tyne Tees airways had already set up the airline's engineering base at the airport with all maintenance and overhaul work being performed. The airfield was also used to store several aircraft of the fleet that weren't in service.

The success of the 1964 air day meant that it became an annual event. For 1965 the organisers had arranged for a Sopwith Pup to give a flying display. However the static display was dominated by a Beverley from the RAF.

In 1966 the flying display included participation by the RAF with a Shackleton, Jet Provost a Whirlwind and the Red Arrows, the show was attended by in excess of 17,000 spectators. The Air Day in 1967 followed much the same format of the previous year. For many the highlight of the 1968 Air Show was the appearance of the North American P-51D Mustang owned by Charles Masefield. A further Air Show was held in 1969, but the only military flying coming from those units of training command based in the area, including Chipmunks and Jet Provosts from Ouston and a Whirlwind from Acklington.

From March 1974 a group of vintage aircraft enthusiasts began to meet at Sunderland Airport. From this informal gathering they formalised as the North East Vintage & Veteran Aircraft Association. (NEVVAA).

On 28 August 1974 the peace of the aerodrome was loudly interrupted when a Royal Air Force Buccaneer strike aircraft carried out an emergency landing on Runway 23 without warning at 14.05. The aircraft had been on its way to carry out a practice attack on a bombing range in Northumberland when it suffered a bird strike. With the navigator injured and the canopy shattered the pilot, an American on an exchange posting, had declared an emergency. The runway at Newcastle had been cleared ready for the aircraft's arrival, when to everyone's surprise the aircraft touched down at Sunderland, even though the runway length was marginal, indeed the aircraft overran the runway. By 1420 an RAF guard had arrived from RAF Ouston with two armourers to make safe four practice bombs. Meanwhile the crew had been taken to hospital by helicopter. By the end of the day the aircraft had been placed in the main hangar. A repair crew arrived and a replacement canopy was flown in by an RAF Andover and the aircraft was repaired and departed, with Sunderland returning to normal.

The last Sunderland Air Day took place in on 15 June 1980 and was perhaps the largest and noisiest display to be held at the airport. The flypast included many RAF aircraft including the Jaguar and Nimrod. Vintage aircraft were represented by the Spitfire, Hurricane and Lancaster with the support of the Firefly, Meteor and Vampire. Many civil residents from the airfield were also displayed.

On 31st May 1984 the airfield was closed after the Sunderland Council reached agreement with a major car manufacturer to sell the site for the creation of a new factory. The future of the museum remains uncertain until late in to the year when the council offers a long term lease on a four acre site just outside the boundary of the former airfield. In 1991 planning permission is granted for a new display hangar.

As of my visit in September 2009 the Museum has the North of England's premier collection of Aviation History and the largest Aviation collection between Yorkshire & Scotland. It is a registered UK charity and is run by enthusiasts and volunteers.

THE FIRST INVESTIGATION

This first investigation is described by Stephen. As always before spending the night on location I research the ghost stories. The first story is of a man called Shaw. Allegedly he died in military action. When his body was removed from the wreckage everything was present except his boots. He is reported to walk around the museum and its hangars. His journey eventually leads him to a workshop where his footsteps can be heard. He then moves into an adjoining canteen to a cupboard containing wreckage believed to be from his plane. There have also been witnesses who have seen black trouser legs with no boots walking around the main hangar. It is also said that Shaw calls out for help and throws things at people to get their attention.

There have also been reports of a man and women talking to each other. They are also thought to be responsible for flashing lights in the hangars. The story here is that the woman was having an affair with a man based at RAF Usworth whilst her husband was away serving in the military. The two in question were both killed in a car crash.

A man called George is also thought to haunt the hangars. He was sunbathing on the roof of one of the hangars when he woke with a start and rolled down to his death. Finally there is the ghost of Frank. Frank had an injured leg and used to get around with the use of a stick. There have been many reports of the click-click as Frank still walks around the hangars today. We arrived at the Museum about 9.30pm. Joining me on the vigil was my girlfriend Pavlina, Wendy and Dan. Also there was Keith a member of staff who worked at the Museum. Our base area was to be the shop of the Museum. Keith showed us many photographs that had been taken on other investigations. They were very good with one showing what appeared to be a girl looking around the side of an aeroplane. Once we got sorted Keith kindly took us on a tour of the site.

There are basically three hangars, a small display area and a workshop. What I would call the main hangar and the biggest is joined onto the display area and shop. The other two step down in size and obviously contain less aircraft because of this. The two smaller hangars are next to each other but are about 50 metres away from the main hangar. Each hangar has a mix of varying aircraft from different generations.

When we arrived back at the shop Keith started to tell us some more of the ghost stories. One of the first stories he told us was of a Czech man called Augustine Preucil. The moment I heard the word Czech I had to stop him and ask if he said Czech. What I didn't mention earlier is that my girlfriend Pavlina is Czech and is obviously fluent at speaking Czech as well as English. When I told Keith this he was very excited. At this point I think Pavlina picked up on what the two of us were thinking. Unfortunately for Pavlina she was going to be calling out in Czech to a Czech spirit. For Pavlina this was her very first night ever on a vigil with me. She had reluctantly agreed to come in the first place so was obviously not too overjoyed at what she would be doing later in the night.

The five of us set off to start the first vigil in the main hangar. It was a totally different spectacle in the dark. It was quite evident that the temperature was getting colder all the time. This being the case I was quite bemused by a warm spot in a certain area. Keith had pointed this out earlier in the night but with it being colder you could feel it more this time around. This warm spot is said to be an area where the ghost of a man is supposed to haunt. I didn't feel scared wandering around in this hangar. I seemed to find myself keep looking for figures standing next to aircraft or trying to spot the legs of Shaw. Just when I started to feel comfortable I did manage to give myself a bit of a fright. I turned to look at something and the circular flag pattern on the side of an old helicopter came into my view for a split second. Instantly without thinking I thought it was a head. I let out a bit of a shout to the amusement of the group. We stayed in this area for a while asking out for spirit activity. Apart from the odd knock and bang you could not be sure if this was just the aircraft cooling down or actually spirits knocking in response to questions. We headed off back to the shop to take a break.

Our next vigil was to take us into what I would call Hangar 2. This was the middle sized of the three on site. As we left the door of the shop Keith told us of a ghostly figure that has been seen looking around the far outside corner of Hangar 1. It was possible to see some sort of black shadow but sceptics would argue this was just a trick of the eye. It was strange none the less. Hangar 2 is the hangar that is supposed to be haunted by the ghost of Czech pilot Augustine Preucil and a girl called Emily. I think now is the time to tell you more about our friend Mr Preucil.

He had been hailed a hero. One of hundreds of Czech pilots who served in the Royal Air Force. He died in an accident over the North Sea on September 18th 1941. He had taken off on a training mission from RAF Usworth with a young Polish pilot. His plane was last seen spiralling towards the water with smoke trailing behind it. A chance discovery did though prove that Preucil did not die that day and was definitely not a hero.

An amateur aviation historian had been sifting through old photographs when he noticed a 1941 picture of a Hurricane on display among other German aircraft. The serial number on the plane was traced and was found to be the same plane Preucil had crashed into the North Sea in 1941.

Preucil was born in Trebsin in what was then Czechoslovakia. He joined the Czech Air Force but when the country went under Nazi control in 1938, he applied to join the Luftwaffe. This was refused on racial grounds. On trying to leave for South America he was arrested at the border. It is thought this is the point he decided or was forced to become a spy.

He was to infiltrate the underground network of Eastern European pilots fleeing to France and Britain. Preucil's escape was staged in Poland and from here he made his way to Britain. He joined the RAF as a pilot. It is believed he deliberately flew poorly so he wouldn't be chosen to fly in combat. This made it easier for him to collect intelligence. It is not known why he chose 1941 to escape. Possibly his mission was complete or was scared of capture. As explained earlier it was believed his plane had crashed into the North Sea. He had though pulled up before hitting the water and headed for Europe. He landed at Ortho in Belgium where a local farmer sheltered him. The following day he approached and chatted to some German soldiers. The farmer was seized and later shot.

Preucil returned to Prague and was given ten thousand Reich marks which was a huge sum of money. He joined the Gestapo and was used to interrogate captured Czech pilots. Many of whom he knew from his time spent in the RAF. His final act of treachery was at a concentration camp at Theresienstadt. He posed as a captured Czech pilot among Czech political prisoners. This is again thought to have cost many of them their lives.

After the war had ended Augustine Preucil was captured in Prague. After a trial in 1947 he was hanged. Keith had informed us from previous investigations that Mediums could sense him in the hangar. Preucil apparently likes to hide in the back corner of it and does not like being disturbed. He does not like the fact that his presence can be sensed by the Mediums and this sometimes led to activity from Preucil. Pavlina, Wendy and I had found ourselves a little bit ahead and moved into the hangar first. We stepped in and all three of us heard a noise from the back of the hangar. The only way I can explain it is that it sounded like a quite loud disgruntled groan. As if it was Preucil telling us to stay away. The hangar itself was square with a large plane positioned across its diagonal, the nose end towards the entry door and the tail end where Preucil is supposed to hide. There is a rope to stop people going too close and a helicopter to the left as you looked down the body of the plane towards the tail. I positioned myself over the rope and past the far wing of the plane and Dan was positioned likewise near the other wing, both of us facing towards where Preucil is supposed to hide. The other three remained behind the viewing rope. We knew from the past that activity had occurred when Preucil had felt threatened. I don't think he or I was prepared for what was going to happen. Pavlina asked out to Augustine in his native language. Through me she was asking him different questions to try and evoke some activity. Pavlina had mentioned to me earlier that to only his friends he would have possibly been called Gusta. I asked for Gusta to try and throw something. He obviously didn't like me calling him Gusta. I heard from near the roof what only could be explained as a popping noise then a split second later something hit the plane in front of me. I don't know if it was aimed at me or not but could not complain as I had asked him to do it. The bang gave us all quite a fright. After we calmed down I started to search for what had been thrown against the plane. After about ten minutes I found a nut and bolt that I believed to be the item thrown. I picked it up and told Pavlina to tell Gusta I am going to throw it back at him. As I went to throw the bolt I heard something whistle past my head and smash on the plane in front of me. I have had things dropped on vigils before but never items aimed at people. Pavlina at this point was close to tears with fear. Believing talking to him in Czech was the catalyst of this activity. Things were starting to get a bit hair raising to say the least. We kept on with questioning but apart from the odd knock or bang did not get anything else thrown at us. I decided to set up a camera on the wing pointing towards where Preucil is supposed to hide. We then set of to go to the smallest of the hangars that is set parallel to Hangar 2.

In Hangar 3 there is table at the front and a single aeroplane at the back. Keith had informed us earlier that the gentleman who was restoring the aeroplane had a heart attack and died whilst working on the plane. It is said if you place your hands on the plane you can make it move. We stood on different sides and placed our hands on the plane. We started to ask out for spirit activity. I have to say that it does feel as though the plane is moving. The feeling was more of a vibration as though there were a small engine inside. We headed from here to the workshop. We held a short vigil in the canteen area but there was no activity. It was decided on the way to collect my camera in Hangar 2 we would try to contact Preucil again. We positioned ourselves much like we had earlier. The room didn't feel as threatening this time. I told Pavlina to tell Augustine that I was going throw something towards where he hides. If he didn't respond then Dan and I would come into the back corner where he hides. I threw the bolt which made an almighty clatter then nearly as soon as the noise had stopped something hit the helicopter next to where Keith, Pavlina and Wendy were standing. This was the sign to say don't come any closer. Pavlina was again quite frightened by this and I decided maybe enough was enough. I decided to call it a day and we headed back to the shop. We never got the chance to try and contact the spirit of Emily the little girl. It is said though that she is frightened of the grumpy man in Hangar 2. Maybe that is why she did not come through. It was a very good night with a few firsts for me. One being the items thrown at me and the other was contacting a spirit using my girlfriend as an interpreter.

The next morning I watched the video from the camera I placed on the wing. The video footage recorded some very strange orbs and bangs. Nobody was in the hangar whilst the camera was recording which makes this all the more puzzling.

NORTH EAST AIR MUSEUM

PART 2

THE INVESTIGATION

The night for this dawned cold but dry. As much of the location was inside large aircraft hangers, as the name suggests, it was hoped the chill would not be too bad. The journey itself for some of the guests and Paul was complicated by the decision of the local council to replace a bridge over a major road. A lorry had damaged it many months ago, the fact that the lorry had a police escort and the police, despite there being a low bridge, had approved the route as safe caused many a smile in the local community.

However, as stated instead of waiting to maybe midnight to close a major road when traffic would be light those geniuses decided peak time on a Saturday night was the preferred time. The resulting torturous detour ensured that Paul, as well as several other guests heading along that same road, arrived a little late. They were however not the last to arrive as one pair managed to head off in completely the wrong direction and it took several calls from Paul to guide them into the right place.

Paul however, found amusement standing at the main gate waiting for the missing couple watching the antics of a drunk who had just left a pub that stood on the same road. Paul watched the drunk spend 10 minutes attempting to light a cigarette and failing as he dropped it numerous times, Paul then watched as the drunk made his way towards Paul weaving from kerb to kerb. Just as he drew level with Paul the drunk startled at noticing this large figure "suddenly" appear in front of him jumped back, tripped and fell. Due to wearing a rucksack on his back and his inebriated state the drunk could do no more than lie on his back legs in the air making vain attempts to get up. Rather like an upside down turtle. After several minutes of being doubled up with laughter, Paul did go and help the man. However, Paul did say it took several attempts to get the drunk on his feet and reasonably steady. At which point the drunk thanked Paul and slowly but deliberately set off back towards the pub, the wrong way. The last Paul saw of him the drunk was heading up a road marked "dead end." However, this all passed the time and at last the missing pair of guest turned up and the night could begin in earnest.

The base room for the investigation was the museum shop; there Keith who was the manager of the museum and the guide for the night met the team. A local BBC radio presenter named Jonathan also joined the teams on the night. This was at Paul's invitation as he was a fan of the show Jonathan hosted and Paul felt his style was perfectly suited to a ghost hunt. A few days prior to the investigation Paul and Stephen had been invited to go to the local BBC station and record an article about their ghost hunting activities and the paranormal in general. That article and the recordings of the night were, once edited, to form the basis of an item on the morning show the Monday following the investigation.

In the shop Paul, being an aviation anorak, was in his element. Thankfully he had left his credit card at home or he would have bought the entire stock of models, books and videos. At last Stephen managed to prise Paul away from the shelves and the usual safety briefing was done to the assembled guests. The only question, which came from Jonathan, was "Will I need to scrape ectoplasm off my Gucci's when I leave?" Not a silly question as he was wearing his Gucci to a ghost hunt in January. However Paul assured him that he would provide him with a "psychic footbath."

The evening started with the group heading into the main hanger that is attached to the shop they were using as a base room. In there the layout was a circle of various exhibits ranging from entire aircrafts through to anti aircraft guns and aero engines. Around the outside of the hanger were various display cases and between the two was a circular aisle.

After the initial familiarization walk around the groups split into four groups and each set off for the corners of the hangers. Once settled and Jonathans Blackberry was prised out of his hand the group began to take it in turns to "call out". As has been explained in other chapters this means simply to ask for any spirit energy present to make themselves known by producing audio or visual phenomenon. Paul himself was instantly drawn to the centre of the room and was aware that the layout of the hanger was "wrong." He said that he felt that the aircraft did not belong there and there should be an aisle down the centre of the hanger. Everything should have been pushed to the sides. Later Keith told him that the site of the hanger, during the time of an active airfield was where rows of huts were. They had been the living quarters for the various personnel, hence Paul's insistence that there should be a centre aisle and everything to each side.

That had been the layout of the huts, however back to the group calling out in the hanger. The first evidence of anything resulting from this was when one of the guests who were paired with Paul suddenly started and hid behind Paul. She had seen what she described as "a large white mist that had come from the centre of the hangers and was floating towards her'. As she watched the cloud grew in size and density she became so scared, she appeared to be trying to push Paul forwards as a sacrifice, as someone would throw some one forward to a hungry lion. The cloud appeared to drift over their heads and disappear. Paul himself could not feel anything from the cloud so was unsure as to what this phenomenon represented but it was as good start to the evening. As the group continued to call out accompanied by the usual barrage of flashes from cameras Paul grew aware of the spirit of a middle-aged man. He wore the uniform of a RAF officer and wore a very distinctive thin and neatly trimmed moustache. The man was not happy at the disruption around what he claimed was "his station." However, his outlook was more of irritation then anger. During this time when Paul was "chatting" with this man the group was continuing to call out.

After the cloud there had been no other signs of any spirit activity. However when one of the groups asked for a sign that they should leave there was immediately a loud bang as one of the doors leading onto the shop slammed shut. As a result of this some people screamed, most jumped and it appeared one guest was running on the spot.

When everyone had settled further attempts were made to get some evidence of the presence of any spirit energies. However, to no avail, one guest did comment that maybe the slamming door was the result of spirit leaving the building. One other odd part of that hanger was that Paul, despite other guest's commenting on the cold, felt he was standing in a warm spot. An oddity that was shown as other guests found his hands and face were noticeably warm to the touch.

However, despite this and it being indoors the cold was intense so it was decided to take a break for a hot drink and that would also give the team the opportunity to check out the door that had slammed. They wanted to see if they could replicate the noise. As always they look for a logical explanation to any activity, looking for a loose catch, draughts or a slipped wedge for example.

As some of the group enjoyed a hot drink and a chat Stephen and a few of the group attempted to make the door slam shut in various ways. By nudging it gently, leaving it open at various angles to see if it would slam or seeking out a reason such as a draught from the main doors. Despite their attempts they could not get the door to slam as loudly or as explosively as it had done. At best it would shut quickly but the "soft close hinges" whose design was aimed at preventing a slam made it impossible to replicate the noise they had all heard. As most of the group had finished their warming drink it was decided to head into a smaller hanger across from the shops location. In that hanger Stephen on his last visit had encountered the energy of a man. That man had much documented history relating to the airfield and at the last visit had shown his anger by tossing stones, bolts and other objects at the team.

None of the team except Stephen and his partner knew of the history but most had heard of their experiences at the last visit and was keen to see what would transpire tonight. Before they ventured out Jonathan unpacked the equipment to be used in the recording. This was nothing more than a large microphone. He then began a rather comical introduction to the next part of the night, concentrating on the fact that on a Saturday night he was freezing in a hanger rather than relaxing on his couch. Once that was completed the team headed towards the infamous hanger.

As they entered Paul was immediately aware of the spirit of a man loitering at the rear of the building. He set off at once toward this man though his progress was hampered due to various bits of airplanes and engines that were laid out in the hanger. Several bruised shins and swear words later he decided he could see fine from where he now was. Behind him Stephen told the group that the corner Paul was heading for was allegedly the same corner that the "stone throwing man" from his past visit hid.

In addition, from his last visit Stephen had learned that the closer he got to that corner the angrier the man got and that had resulted in the stones and bolts being thrown at the team. The team tonight had a unique advantage, as this man was Czech. As is Stephens partner Pavlina. So rarely we had a ghost was being addressed in his own language that was not native to the rest of the group.

As Pavlina began to ask for evidence of the man's presence and Stephen headed towards the corner to further provoke a response Paul noticed a strange thing. The man rather than acting aggressively was retreating away as Stephen approached and was running away as fast as he could. In no way was he displaying any aggression nor did he appear to want to throw anything at the team. As Paul watched him sidle along the hanger wall he began to follow him, which appeared to even further unnerve the man. It was also odd the Keith the museum manager called out that he could see the man heading in the same direction that Paul knew he was moving. It seemed that Keith has some mediumship talent.

It was also odd that the Czech man would not leave the walls of the hanger. In all his attempts to escape the attention of the team not once did he attempt to cross the centre of the room. After around ten minutes of Stephen calling out, Pavlina asking for evidence in the man's native language without there being any response the man had ended up back in the corner where he started. After a brief consultation between Paul and Stephen it was decided to reverse their roles and positions. Paul would edge towards the location on the Czech pilot and Stephen would block his escape route. As they moved into position Paul could see this was unnerving the pilot, he appeared to be very edgy. Possibly as he now realized that Paul was a medium and could see him. Though Paul approached the man and his corner in a completely unthreatening manner, stressing that he and the team were here simply for knowledge the pilot was still not happy. To the extent that as aircraft blocked his sight of the pilot now and then stones or bolts started to fly towards Paul.

There were several that seemed to be aimless in their aim, simply appearing to bounce off bits and bobs in the middle of the hanger. One however landed with a loud thud only inches from where Paul was standing. What was even more astonishing is judging by the sounds whatever had been thrown appeared to first bounce of an aircrafts hood before bouncing along the wing towards Paul. As has been stated before Paul is unusual as a medium as he will always look for logical reasons for any happenings such as this. Later Paul said that any of the other objects that sounded like they could have been thrown, possibly could have fallen after being dislodged due to a group of people moving around in the dark, even so, many appeared to come directly from overhead so even that is unlikely. However, the object that bounced off the planes cowling and skittered along the wing was thrown! Since there was no one from the group standing anywhere near where the object came from the only conclusion was that it was the pilot trying to warn Paul off.

Anyone that knows Paul will understand that backing off from a threat is not in his nature, so he continued his approach towards the man and the corner he was standing. As Paul neared the corner and at last he could see clearly as no longer was his vision blocked by aircraft he could see that the pilot was no longer throwing anything but was extremely frightened. He was crouched on the floor in a foetal position and obviously terrified, so scared that Paul could get no sense from him. Hoping that he would respond to his own language he asked Pavlina to inquire why the man was so afraid. Paul saw that as Pavlina spoke the pilot started at hearing his mother tongue again. However even then all Paul could get from the man was a garbled mix of English and what he assumed was Czech and the pilot appeared to be defending himself. Even after several attempts at trying Paul couldn't make any real sense of the man's ravings other than he appeared to be afraid of the judgment from his own people. Paul was not sure if that meant his native countryman, the English or even his fellow pilots.

Since it was obvious to Paul that there was little chance of any coherent communication with the pilot, nor that he appeared to want any help from Paul he asked the group to leave the hanger, at least for the time being to leave the pilot in peace. As the group started to file out the hanger Paul watched the pilot as he slowly uncurled and stood.

What was also amazing was the way his demeanour changed and he appeared to be smirking and contemptuous of the group. Paul felt that the pilot felt he had won somehow. Once again due to the cold a quick break was called for so a return to the shop was in order. Once there Keith told of a third hanger where he would like the group to participate in an experiment. He would not say anymore but as it was an intriguing statement, the group was happy to go for it. The hanger was located at the far edges of the museums ground but still only a short walk. As the group headed over to the hanger they all passed a Canberra aircraft that is parked outside as part of the museum's exhibits.

As Paul approached he commented that he could see streams of men walking back and forth between the main hanger and the hanger they were heading for. Not active spirit but a memory of what used to be the day-to-day life on the location. Keith told him that in fact that area used to be the route to the canteen and there would have been a constant stream of personnel coming and going over that ground when the site was operational.

When Keith finished telling Paul all that, they entered the hanger that Keith wanted the group to try his experiment. As they did Paul became aware of a spirit man standing at the tail of a jet plane within the hanger. Oddly, as far as Paul was concerned was the uniform the man was wearing. It was not the light blue of a RAF pilot, the man was a pilot, but instead a dark blue almost black. Upon querying this with the man Paul was shown a mental image of the aircraft in front of him landing on a ship and the words "Fleet Air Arm."

Paul thanked the man for the information then switched his attention to Keith who was explaining to the group "the experiment." It was quite a simple one, he asked the entire group to place their fingers lightly on the fuselage of the aircraft in front of them and report what happened. Keith was also very insistent that there were an equal number of people down each side. Paul suspected that this was to be an experiment in psychometry but he was to be surprised. With everyone except Keith touching the aeroplane he began to ask the spirit man to show that he was present, the same spirit man that Paul had conversed with when he entered the hanger. Slowly but most definitely everyone reported feeling the body of the aeroplane begin to vibrate. As Keith continued to ask the pilot to keep showing his presence in this unique way the vibrations increased until there was a definite throbbing coming from the body of the plane. The best way to describe it is as though there was a small engine running within the body. That was not happening, as the aircraft was only a shell, however as the group continued to experience these odd vibrations Paul again began to communicate with the pilot. The pilot told Paul his name was Peter and he showed Paul that the aircraft everyone was touching had at one time been damaged. The tail section was mangled in some way, the pilot Peter did not say how. As the vibrations through the aircraft slowed and stopped the group gathered around to compare notes and Paul could see that the pilot was still standing at the rear of the aircraft quite happy to observe the group but no desire to communicate directly.

This was a first for Paul, though Stephen had experienced this at his previous visit to the museum. As always though Paul had not been made aware of the history of the location nor any reported paranormal activity. Paul did comment later that he really did not know what to make of the whole thing. As he did put it, "How can you explain a full size jet vibrating?" Hardly can anyone say as they often do with Ouija boards that someone was pushing it." There were other spirit people within the hanger that appeared to be just getting on with businesses. Two people in particular were busy working on a fire engine from the same era as the jet but were not interested in the group and ignored Paul's attempts to ask questions of them. The group did attempt briefly to hold a séance and some table tipping in the room but there was no movement from the table or any other contact. Therefore, you guessed it, back to the base room shop for a hot drink.

On route to the base room it was suggested that it would be a good idea to grab a picture of Paul and Stephen standing with Jonathan next to the Canberra aircraft. However as they posed the main light over the hanger they had just left went out. It was movement activated but it was needed to provide extra light as well as the flash to get a good picture.

Therefore, the only way to keep the light on was of course to have someone moving near it. It was therefore with great amusement that Paul tried to pose for the picture while watching his daughter and her partner, both had joined the guest list for the night, both dressed in many layers to ward off the cold, walking around waving their arms looking like overweight Weebles. In fact so comical was the sight it took several minutes for the group to compose themselves by which time the light went off again. So the whole cycle began again but at last the combination of waving Weebles, the light and a none corpsing Paul combined and the shot was taken. Pity that there had not been some forethought as a video of the sight would have been a sure thing for one of the "home viewers tapes" TV programs. Once again the whole group gathered in the base room and with fingers wrapped around hot drinks the game plan for the rest of the investigation was decided. Jonathan had to leave the group now, he had an early start the next day and he felt he had enough for the show.

Stephen was very keen to go back into the smaller hanger where the objects were thrown. So it was agreed to split into two groups. Stephen and his partner along with another guest would head for that hanger and Paul and the rest would have another walk around the large hanger behind the shop area. Stephens group in the smaller hanger were again a little disappointed at the level of activity, while there were a few bangs and cracks it was as Stephen said "hard to be sure if they were not just the usual night time sounds. Though again objects were being thrown occasionally. Paul's group headed into the larger hanger along with Keith the manager. Just inside the entry door Keith stopped and asked Paul if he was picking up on anything, Paul was still sensing the same officer he had picked up on during the early walk around of the hanger. But as he stood he started to pick up the sensations of sitting in the cockpit of an aircraft that was spinning out of control.

Paul reported that he could sense the aircraft spiralling

towards the ground in an anti clockwise direction. He was in the pilot's seat and could feel him fighting with the stick and the rudder pedals trying to correct the spin but feeling his input on the stick was having no effect. This feeling carried on for several moments till it felt to Paul that the man impressing these sensations on Paul felt he had got the message over. Then Paul kept on hearing the words "it was not my fault" repeated over and over again with a great stress on the word "my fault". Paul was relaying all this out loud to the group and Keith in particular was listening with great intensity.

At last when Paul had passed over all the information he had been given Keith borrowed a torch and stepped over the barriers separating the walkway and the exhibits. When he returned he had with him a board display that had been hidden under a sheet. On it was the tale of a pilot called Shaw, unknown to Paul the tale of this pilot is part of the museums history. Keith told Paul the story that Shaw, a young pilot when the area was an operational airfield was killed as a result of a mid air collision. He had spun into the ground but the other pilot had managed to land.

As the tale was being told and Keith got to the point in the story that told of Shaw been blamed for the accident once again he came through to Paul insisting, "It was not my fault". It appeared this was the main reason for his communication with Paul he wanted to make it clear that he was not at fault. In fact he insisted that if he had not taken the action that ended up costing him his life both pilots would have lost their life. After Keith had finished telling the tale to the group Paul commented that he found it odd that the pilot Shaw had been so strong in his presence when the accident and the airfield was located quite some distance from where they now stood. With that Keith reached over and lifted a tarpaulin to reveal some aircraft pieces and told the group that it was parts from the wreckage of Shaw's aircraft. The rest of the time spent in that hanger was of little interest with no other activity. Stephen appeared in the hanger with the suggestion that he and Paul swap locations. He did say that there was some sort of activity going on in the smaller hanger, the one where the Czech pilot was supposed to haunt. Things being quiet that seemed a good idea and Paul headed for that hanger. As he approached he found Pavlina and a guest waiting outside standing in what was now a fine rain. They claimed they did not wish to be in the hanger without Paul being with them. Odd as Stephen had felt there was not a huge amount of activity nor had he felt it was a particularly threatening atmosphere. They did say that it had been very active, with noises and they thought something being thrown at them. As they entered Paul immediately got the overwhelming emotion of resentment flooding towards him from the Czech pilot who was standing at the far end of the hanger. Paul at once now understood why the level of activity was so high in this area when Stephen and Pavlina were present together. The Czech pilot resented the relationship between Pavlina a Czech woman and Stephen, an English man. Just in the same way that American pilots encountered hostility from English males during the Second World War while stationed in the UK, so the Czech pilot was not happy that Pavlina was dating an Englishman. Hence whenever they were together he wanted to make his resentment and displeasure clear. This explains why so often the missiles thrown by the pilot seemed to be aimed at Stephen. Just as this "conversation" was ending Stephen and the rest of the group entered the hangar. Upon their entry there was at once a feeling of petulance coming from the pilot, though he did not react in any other way, seeming to almost decide to ignore everything that was going on around him.

As a final attempt to see if the team could prompt some more activity from the pilot it was agreed to form a circle and hold another séance. Despite taking another tack this time and attempting to empathize with the pilot now feeling that there was a greater understanding of the reason for his resentment there was no further activity.

As the group was leaving after this failed attempt Paul did notice two men working in another part of the hanger and he was given the distinct impression that they used to be volunteers at the museum, rather than fitters when the location was an operational station. Keith later confirmed that that area was only used by the museum for repairing aircraft and not during the active period of the site. As they were making their way back to the base room Paul was stopped in his tracks by the mental image of a man falling from a hanger roof.

Though he did feel it was an event associated with the time that the airfield was operational rather than as a museum. He could not tell where or which hanger as it was only a brief flash. Not being able to shed any further light on that event it is noted simply for reference. It now being close to 2.30 AM and as the cold, if it was possible, was growing more intense it was universally agreed to end the night then. So as usual all equipment was stored and a sweep of the base area was made to ensure it was left in a tidy condition. Keith opened the entry gates that were always kept locked and after thanking him the team headed for home.

The following Monday Jonathan broadcast the edited portions of both the night and his recording of his interview with Paul and Stephen. As maybe is to be expected the experience with the "vibrating jet" was the lasting impression that he took from the night. It was certainly the highlight for all the other guests if the feedback on the "fans" page is to be believed. It is most definitely the hardest one for any sceptics to explain. So that is the sum total of the North East Aircraft Museum. The only other thing worth mentioning is Paul still complains that he was not allowed to "play" in the cockpits of any of the aircraft.

He may stop sulking soon.

HIGH HEAD CASTLE

THE HISTORY

High Head Castle is a large fortified manor house in the English county of Cumbria. It is located between Carlisle and Penrith. The house is now little more than a ruin with just the mere exterior walls and certain foundations surviving. It is currently privately owned, and the owners have now for some time been trying to restore it to its former glory.

The Kings Castle in the Forest of Inglewood originally occupied the site. The earliest written record is of the original castle is from 1272. This castle was a medieval square pele tower within a curtain wall.

The first known occupants of the house were the Richmond family who bought and extended the house in the 16th century. Only its western wing remains, with its unmistakable straight headed mullioned windows with round-arched lights under hood moulds, although attached to the south-west corner of this wing is the basement of a square tower which presents evidence of 14th century work.

The house was later sold to the Baron Brougham and Vaux who made some alterations. One member of the family, H. Richmond Brougham, had a new facade built in 1744-8. It is eleven bays long, with a pedimented three-bay centre, and a walled front garden with coupled Ionic columns. When the Broughams no longer required the house they rented it out for some time. The only known people to have rented it were the Cavaghan family (co-founders of Cavaghan & Gray) who lived in the house for around three years during the thirties. The castle was largely destroyed by fire in 1956, and is now little more than a shell. According to one account this was put out by the fire brigade, but nor before it had been whipped up by gales into 100ft high flames which destroyed the roof. The next day, it is said, fire started again in the castles smouldering shell. The fire was eventually put out by lunchtime that day, but it was too late. Both the medieval wing and the principal house are Grade 2 listed.

Adjacent is a fine stable quadrangle with heavy rustication, a steep pediment gable and cupola.

THE INVESTIGATION

The opportunity to investigate this location came about as a result of Stephen's business relationship with Christopher who also owns Brougham hall. You will recall if you read that chapter that it was said that the name of the location would have to be kept a secret. Now the investigations were done and dusted permission was given to reveal the location. Paul and Stephen were incredibly fortunate, as this location had never been investigated before. This within the world of paranormal investigation is a coup of huge proportions. Not only were Stephen and Paul excited about this opportunity but so was the owner Christopher Terry. He said via E mail: "Remember, you are the first paranormal investigators ever to come to High Head, which is considerably older than Brougham. It will be fascinating to know what you manage to discover."

Due to the sensitivity of the location, there were homes nearby on the estate and the secrecy needed on the location and the building, it was decided that only selected guests would be invited to attend this event. It is a testament to the loyalty and respect that Paul and Stephen have built with their regular clientele that they were willing to book and pay for an event without having anything except sketchy details of where they were going, or what they were to face. The only information supplied was the date and the county.

As the site of High Head is quite hard to find Stephen decided to arrange a meet up at a public location and have people follow him to the site. He scoured the local area via maps and on line satellite pictures and found a car park that was ideally located. So two days prior to the event E-mails were dispatched to the guests with detailed information on the meet up location and also at last the site they were going to investigate. Everything was in place ready for the investigation on a Saturday night in late February.

Paul and Stephen met up early to travel together and go over plans for the night. As the meet up point was about a 90-minute drive from their homes they set off around 7pm. However on route one of Stephens's friends who was a last minute booking for this event telephoned. In between bouts of laughter he informed Stephen that his choice of meet up location, the car park, was known locally as a well-known site for "dogging." (Anyone innocent of that term should search the net for more information.) But suffice to say it involves acts normally reserved to take place between loving couples in private but not as a rule a car park.

Stephen was a little worried about this information but Paul was barely able to stifle an uncontrollable outburst of giggles. Upon arrival they found their guests waiting as well as several other cars. One in particular had its interior light on which showed three youngish men all drinking lager from cans and smoking what were obviously "herbal" cigarettes.

As Paul emerged from the car in his usual outfit of cut off T-shirt, leather waistcoat, jeans and paratrooper boots and ambled over to where the guest's cars were parked there was an immediate reaction. The interior light of the young lad's car was switched off, windows were wound up and there was the distinctive "click" as doors were locked. Although amused and sorely tempted to go tap on the window Paul instead greeted the guests and fired up the Sat Nav for the final leg of the journey.

So it was a convoy of 4 fully laden vehicles that set off following Stephen who was driving and Paul who was navigating. Though both had visited the site before in daylight it was still a hard place to find. But thanks to the rolling Sat Nav, a map and Stephens pre prepared directions they managed to reach the site without problems.

However, on arrival some of the guests expressed concern as the only way out now when the event ended was to reverse back up the track they had came down. All of course in pitch darkness and having to avoid a drainage ditch that flanked the left hand side. However that was to be faced later.

So they all decamped and grouped together and followed Stephen towards the hall with Paul bringing up the rear ensuring that no one was lost en route. The sight that faced them was of a large building, much of it now derelict following a fire in the 1950s but still an imposing building. If anyone wished to have a visual representation to sum up a "haunted house" then this building's façade would be an ideal image. The base room for the night was located on the one remaining floor of the building that was now safe to enter. Inside chairs had been set up and small tea light candles flickered in the room as illumination. As the room had a vaulted ceiling that had the original stonework even this room was striking.

Stephen set off to meet up with Christopher while Paul spent some time chatting to the guests. In the initial invitation to the guests it had been emphasised that this location was most defiantly an "Extreme Location". There was no electricity, no toilets, no heating and much of both the interior and exterior of the site was overgrown. Admittedly at the end of the night that many of the other guests had enjoyed the hospitality of the "catering crew" as Paul dubbed them... more on them later.

However, everyone wanted to get on with the business in hand, ghost hunting. The group was split into two parties. Though the estate is quite large, the parts of the building that were safe to enter were quite close together. Basically all the rooms led off the one corridor. However before they all set off Paul and Stephen offered some further safety advice to the group. This was in addition to the usual talk as so much of this location was outdoors, overgrowing with weeds and brambles and there were also steep drops to a river in some parts of the site. In addition Paul said that as he had experienced strong impressions on his daytime walk around he was going to take a bit of a back seat on this investigation and see what data was forthcoming from the guests. So one group stayed in the interior of the building while the others went off to explore the grounds that included a small maze, a terraced garden, a small grotto or summer house and a large field that we were told had some history. What that history was only Stephen and Christopher the owner knew. In this chapter we shall be combining all the information gathered by all the guests and presenting it to you room-by-room, or area-by-area if outdoors. So either group may have gleaned the information. However, after the initial safety briefing and introductory walk around some of the guests surprised Paul and Stephen. Most of the guests returned to their cars to gather spare clothing, it was already below freezing, spare batteries, cameras plus whatever food and hot drinks they had brought. But one group who had travelled together surpassed anyone's supplies. They arrived back at the base room laden with bags of sandwiches, cakes, biscuits and supplies of tea, coffee and milk. Paul watched fascinated as they then produced flasks and a camping stove and proceeded to brew a cuppa. Though they had been told it was an extreme location Paul did feel as though he had wandered into the base camp for an assault on Everest. However he did muse that maybe they had got it right and he also as has been said dubbed them "the catering crew."

THE BASE ROOM

The first information that was imparted was in fact on the room that was made the base room. Upon first entering the room one guest said at once that she felt tipsy, slightly drunk. In fact even to the casual observer the change in her personality was plain. She was by nature and outgoing woman but now she was almost at the, "you're my best mate" stage of drunkenness. Thankfully this only lasted for a few minutes and she was able to recover. Upside of psychic drunkenness is no hangover of course.

Over the course of the night during breaks and also while sitting in small groups many of the guests picked up on the same or similar bits of information. It was said that a "nice lady" was prevalent in this room. She wore a white mop cap and was described as "bustling around" the room as well as up and down the corridor outside the room. Several of the guests picked up on the name Mary, though one felt it was Molly. It seemed the reason for one of the guests feeling slightly intoxicated was that this woman Mary had a habit of sampling some liquor that was being used as an ingredient in the cooking.

One woman guest described it as being a "Sweet plum flavoured drink." No one felt they could put a name to the drink, or even think of a modern equivalent. But as the year of 1786 was felt to be the time this women was alive it may have been a drink favoured at that time but now passed from popularity. They also felt that there was the spirit energy of a young girl who came and went, as well as playing in the corridor. She was said to look to be about 8 years old and described as "A happy soul."

Later when you read of the energies that were encountered in the corridor you will see that some people felt this might have been a male child.

THE FIRST SEANCE

At Paul's suggestion the first séance was held in a room at end of the corridor nearest the present owner's cottage and to the rear of the building. The reason for this was Paul at his last brief visit had picked up on an energy there and wanted to see what information came through. The owner had already left out chairs and a semi circle of people was made. After leaving some time for everyone's eyes to grow adjusted to the darkness Paul started the séance and asked for people's impressions. Many of the guests told of sensing a man named Gregory (this matched the name Paul had picked up on during his visit). Of the guests sensing this man, over half of them felt he was not a pleasant person. Almost universally he was described as being a sly person who loved to intimidate people. He constantly felt the other staff was talking and plotting against him, as a result his habit was to eavesdrop on all the other staff. Paul said he saw him as a man with lank longish hair. He was dressed in an outfit of breeches, waistcoat and brown shin high boots. All the guests felt that this man was annoyed at the presence in the area that he felt was his domain. Paul could see him pacing around the semi circle of people with what looked like growing impatience.

As Paul watched the man and his pacing some of the guest commented that the room if it was possible seemed to be growing darker and colder. One guest complained off feeling an icy breeze blowing across her face. Oddly the people either side of her could feel nothing even though they tried moving their faces in line with hers to try and pick up on any draughts. Another guest said they had caught sight of this man as he had first entered the room and described him as "a dark figure." Paul unknown to the other guests had picked up on some other information on his first visit relating to this man and a young girl from the corridor. Paul began to ask for the man to make his presence known by making a sound, touching people or throwing an object at them. Receiving no response to these requests, Paul after 10 minutes or so decided to see how the man would react to him revealing the information he had picked up on. When Paul did quietly but firmly start to talk of this man and the little girl and how the man had been part of a disaster blamed on the little girl, there was almost an instant reaction.

Many of the guest said they began to hear the words "GET OUT" screamed at them. A notebook held by one of the guests sitting opposite Paul was wrenched out her hands and thrown to the floor in the middle of the circle. As Paul continued to talk of the man, about the little girl and his "crime" he became even more agitated. Once again it was a female guest, who while asking questions of the man and his links to the little girl, suddenly yelped. She had felt her right ear being pulled hard and twisted. So hard to be very painful and upon inspection later there was a very distinct red mark. As the group continued to ask of this man a reason for his actions and daring him to show himself or prove of his existence, a male guest to the left of Paul began to choke. After a short but intense mental battle of wills the man was able to breath and claimed that he had felt cold hands around his throat strangling him. Paul double-checked that everyone wanted to continue, however, it seemed that the man had given up.

The man had attempted to intimidate the group and when even a physical attack had failed, he had left the room showing he was still the coward that many felt he had been. However most people felt he was still lurking in the corridor. Two guests felt the date of 1856 was particularly important around the spirit energy of this man. After he had left, the room appeared to warm up and a woman with a P initial with a Petula sounding name popped into her head. She, it was felt, worked in or had some connection to the kitchen, there was also a large dog present, though no one could identify the breed nor if it was connected to any other energy. As activity appeared to have peaked in that room it was felt it was a good time to end the séance and withdraw to the base room to make further plans. So Paul shut down the circle and the group decamped to have a hot drink.

NB. Later after reading this account the owner of the hall Christopher told that a young girl was thought to be responsible for a fire that destroyed most of the building

THE CORRIDOR

This corridor ran the full width of the building and no doubt when the castle hall was in use it would have been a hive of activity. To some degree it was the same on the night of the investigation. Many people picked up on how the atmosphere would have felt like at the time that the hall was a place full of activity. How the corridor would have looked if you were standing as an invisible observer. There was the impression of much hustle and bustle and many of the characters we have already mentioned, such as Gregory were also apparent moving through the corridor. There was also the impression of lots of children playing in that area. The team had no idea why children would have been playing in an area that would have been a workplace but the sounds and feeling of children's laughter, screams of delight and chatter was picked up by some people. As mentioned before in the base room part of this chapter some guests were picking up feelings of a young boy and others a young girl. At first it was assumed there were two spirit energies in that area but when the descriptions of the clothing started to tally from each group that theory was dismissed. What was apparent was this child had ringlets spilling down both sides of the face. The brown hair was set in a very stylish manner, not in any way a natural style. This may explain the confusion between the two groups as this image could easily have been interpreted as male or female by anyone who was only seeing that particular image. Some mediums for example will see in their minds eye a full body image of the spirits energy, others only the head and shoulder. But what was apparent to all, even those only seeing the head and shoulders was the sense of quality breeding attached to this child.

People agreed that the style and quality of the clothing worn by this youngster as well as the air of breeding indicated that it did not belong in what was a servant's area, possibly a child from "upstairs" who liked to come down to this area to play, for what reason was not known. Some of the guest did pick up on the name Kennedy linked to this child and the time period of 1777. Lastly there was also picked up by a couple of guests the spirit energy of a man. He was described as having a wispy beard and wore a leather apron with hoops attached to it. The name of Albert was connected to this man, his name it was assumed. It was felt that he was sneaking towards the wine cellar. For what reason is not known but most people described his manner as "furtive."

OUTSIDE THE BUILDING

We shall be returning to some other rooms inside the building later but at the moment lets us look at some of the activity and the sensations that were felt and seen outside the building. Some of the information relates to activity within the grounds themselves and some to activity that was observed going on inside the derelict areas of the building observed by the team members from outside the building.

First let us look at the rear of the building and also an area set into the cliffs below the rear of the building. That has been described as a grotto or summerhouse. But it is basically an area carved into the cliffs that would have given a cool space to sit during hot summer months. Only 4 of the guests decided to risk the steep path that led down to this area. They held a short vigil and did experience some light anomalies that were hard to explain, many orbs were also picked up in the photographs that they took but the felt that this was simply down to dust. The main anomaly that was curious and hard to explain was a light that seemed to move around the group, disappearing and reappearing seemingly at random, though it did seem to favour one guest in particular. The whole area though was felt to be so calm and pleasant that had the weather been better and warmer many of them could have stayed there some considerable time. However as the temperature was sitting around freezing they returned to the rest of the group and continued exploring the rest of the estate.

At the rear of the building, above the grottos, it was possible to see into what were once grand rooms. Though the grandeur is now gone and some rooms were almost over taken by the weeds and small tress that now grew it is still evident that this was once an impressive area. Two guests independently described as seeing/sensing that there should have been an archway set into the stone in the middle of the façade. There were no signs evident in the wall that remains and it was not possible to establish a time frame for this feature. It will be interesting to see if any readers have any knowledge of this feature. There was also a room that several people described as "being a place of rest and prayer."

Once gain there were two independent reports of guests seeing a woman praying in that area. So it seems at one time that that area of the building did have some religious use. Who the woman was or why she was praying is unknown. Most of the guests however also said how at peace they felt in the whole area at the rear of the building. They variously describe it as "tranquil, peaceful and spiritual."

FRONT OF BUILDING

The front of the hall overlooks a small maze, small both in area and in the height of the hedges. After the maze is a large grassed area with some private homes to the left of the lawn and to the right there is a series of steps that lead onto a gate then on to a walled garden. At the top of the grassed area is the entry track to the hall and to one side of that a stile. Over the stile is a large area of grass, trees and ditches as well as the other side of the wall surrounding the walled garden. We shall return briefly to all these areas, except of course the private homes later.

In the meantime, let us return to the area in front of the castle, the maze and also a short path leading along the front of the castle. Within the maze one guest had the impression of there being lots of sneaking around and whispering in the portion of the maze to the left of the castle as you face the building. On the grassed, lawn area many of the guests had impressions of "gaiety." This is a very old fashioned word for anyone to use in modern days terms. Many guests had the impression of this area being the scene for many parties and celebrations. The older version of the modern barbeque shall we say. They said they could see women in, "crinoline dresses and bustles," even though the one guest who had the strongest impression of this scene had no idea what those terms meant. But it was not only women who people felt enjoyed being in this area.

There was also the feeling of men strolling in the area wearing tailored suits and cravats, again a contrast maybe to the modern day outdoor party attire of shorts and T shirts. It seems that even when having fun there were still standards to be observed. Though what it must have felt like for both sexes to be so heavily bundled up in clothes in the summer heat while trying to look "cool" is hard to imagine.

As many guests also had the feelings and impressions of the area being used to play croquet and tennis one cannot only imagine how hard it would have been to play while dressed in what would now be considered formal clothes. In the area of the lawn that leads off into a walled garden one guest had the feeling of there being seats, music and laughter. It seems that many areas on the estate was set aside purely for the enjoyment of the owners and their guests. The area near the walled garden was felt also to have had seating and been an area where people could go to sit in the shade, to escape the heat of the midday sun maybe.

Oddly Paul later said that in the area of the maze his only impression was of a feeling of water. This was at odds with all the other guests' feelings and rather strange. But further research may shed light on that. It was obvious in all areas of this building that there was the feeling of layers of history and activity. As though some parts of the present day building had once been part of another structure. But a structure that would be best described as having a completely different use. However the team next turned their attention to the front of the building.

Much of it now is simply a façade following a fire but parts of the ground floor, the main area of investigation by the team, was still intact. Above the entrance to that lower area was once the main door into the hall. Taking that entrance as a reference point, two of the guests described seeing a woman standing in the 2nd window to the left on the first floor. Both described her as a very well dressed woman with brown hair set in ringlets wearing what they described as "a bonnet." Once again we get the description of hair being in ringlets as we did with the child in the corridor. It is not known if this was simply a common style of hair over a period or if this was in fact the grown up young girl that was seen in the corridor. Mainly as this woman seemed to not want to make any contact with the team, some of the group were mediums and they did "ask" this woman for information but to no avail, she seemed content to simply observe the comings and goings. She appeared to be curious and was seen to be "curtain twitching", moving the curtain to one side, to watch the various members of the team as they moved around the pavement at the front of the building. In the window next to that but nearer the main door there was seen to be standing a tall elegant gentleman who was well dressed and described as "distinguished."

He too appeared to be only wishing to watch the activities of the team and ignored all attempts from some guests to communicate. But many felt that this was due to him being rather snobbish and simply not feeling that it would have been appropriate for him to talk to the lower orders. Some of the guests from observing the style of dress of this man felt he would have been from the 1800s. Though none of the team had any specialist knowledge on this topic it is not clear why they felt this or how they would know what 1800 dress sense would look like. Maybe as often is the case impressions are given by the spirit people.

THE RIGHT OF THE BUILDING

To the right side of the hall as you face it is the cottage that is the home of the site owner. This then leads onto the side of the hall that was the outer wall to the corridor previously described in this chapter. Here there was a small-grassed area that drops down via a very steep and inaccessible bank to a river that encircles that side and the rear of the castle. The river itself is some 75 feet below this grassed area and was clearly heard but given the darkness and the depth it was not possible to see it.

Some parts of this area has no barrier to prevent people stumbling over the edge down as has been said is a very steep bank down to the river. So both Paul and Stephen were at great pains to warn guests of the danger as well as keeping sight of everyone. In one particular part of this area, at the very rear of the building where if access was possible you would be turning the corner onto the rear of the hall, many people felt that they were being drawn or pushed towards the edge of the drop. One guest in particular seemed to be very strongly affected. Paul was watching her closely as he sensed her unease and trepidation. At one time Paul described her as looking as though she had a very strong wind pushing her towards the edge of the bank that in that area would be more accurately described as a cliff.

She was standing with legs braced and arms outstretched seeming trying to resist a force that wanted to push her over the edge. As has been said Paul was watching her very carefully and stayed at hand in case he needed to grab her and pull her back from the edge. However after a little while she seemed to gain control and was able to back away from the edge to safety. She described the experience as though there was a huge force trying to throw her off her feet and over the edge of the cliff. What was even odder was that she said it did not feel as though it was a human. She felt it was not hands that were attempting to push her to the cliff edge but just a "force" that she could not explain. Others described seeing a large man with bad breath who they felt was the reason people were feeling pushed towards the drop but this was not the case with this guest.

200

Other guests had the same sort of feeling though to a lesser degree and had no problems with staying well back from the cliff edges. Why this particular guest was affected so strongly is not known though it was obvious even to the casual observer that she had to use all her strength to resist the force she described.   It could have been that she was simply more sensitive to this "force" though that is simply speculation. Lastly in this area people described seeing a large dog that reminded them of a wolfhound.

As there was also description of a large dog in the corridor area that was on the other side of the wall in this area it may have been the same dog. As it was a very clear and frosty night it was felt by the team that a break for a hot drink was a good idea so they all returned to the base room to go over plans for the rest of the night. Back at the base room the "catering crew" once again sprang into action. The kettle was soon whistling, plastic boxes of sandwiches, cakes, biscuits and scones were unpacked and generously passed around all the other guests. The ginger cake was Paul's particular favourite. So through mouthfuls, plans for the rest of the night were hatched.   Stephen who as always was privy to information kept hidden from Paul and the other guests asked for a group to spend some time in a area off the corridor leading from the entry point the team had used into the building. Some of the guests voiced the opinion that they had ventured into that room briefly during the walk around and thought it was a lovely warm room. Stephen said nothing simply saying he would love some feedback. So once the midnight feast was done and dusted Paul led a bunch of guests towards that room.

THE GUARD ROOM

The title giving to this part of the chapter is simply as a result of information that was later told to Stephen. There were about 10 people in the group and they entered the room and formed a loose circle. Once everyone was happy, torches were turned off and darkness settled itself on the room. Almost instantaneously the atmosphere of the room altered. The warm and friendly room people had described disappeared as the torches were turned off and a man made his presence known. Paul who as previously stated had planned to take a back seat in this investigation at this point spoke up. He sensed a very large Scotsman, though he did base that assumption purely on this man's attire. He was wearing a dirty white shirt and a kilt worn of course around his waist but also with parts of it draped over his shoulder. The colour and pattern of the garment drew Paul. It seemed to be of large tartan check but the colours, particularly the red on it, was very vivid. Paul felt that this sort of vivid colour maybe appropriate in today's time period. It seemed odd for the era that this man was clearly from. To Paul it looked artificial. But was in no doubt was the aggression and hostility of this man; he seemed to ooze hatred and hostility. He at once made a beeline for Paul and stood very close, even though Paul is 6 foot tall and a large man he felt this man tower above him. It seems that even from the spirit world Paul draws the "nutter" types to him.

What also became apparent was the incredible stench coming from this man's body odour. It was so foul that Paul was struggling not to retch; he felt instinctively that this man would take this as a sign of weakness. As the man was standing so close it was also obvious was that his breath was equally rank. The man continued to attempt to intimidate Paul by standing very close, moving into what would be considered personal space and glaring at Paul exuding a hostile and aggressive aura. Once Paul had recovered himself, he learned to breathe through his mouth and not his nose to avoid the rank odours coming from the man. He was equally aggressive in his stance towards the man. Paul took a step closer to the man to indicate he was more than happy to go head to head in what could only be a battle of wills. Oddly despite this man's aggression, Paul at no time felt he was in any physical danger. As all this was happening Paul was keeping up a running commentary describing the pictures, smells and emotions he was experiencing as well as the man's manner. At this point a picture of the room in another time was implanted in Pauls mind. Whether this was a memory of the room or it was something that this man could do is unknown. In the room at the rear Paul was shown a brazier full of glowing coals. In there was at first what Paul thought was pokers to tend the fire. However it became obvious that in fact there were iron used to brand people as a form of torture. As Paul was seeing this image, but before he had a chance to pass on this information to the rest of the group with him, one of the guests said he could smell a barbecue. With that information Paul decided to hold his counsel and see what other information was brought up.

Other people in the group started to agree with the smell of barbecue but they had put it down to something eaten during the break. But it was quickly pointed out that though a stove was used in the break it was only to boil a kettle. Everything else was eaten cold. Then a guest said she could see a "basket full of coals with rod sticking out". When asked to further describe the image it became apparent it was the same picture that Paul was presented with but he had not told anyone of. As the rest of the group was digesting this information another guest complained that she felt as though she had been burned on the neck and she felt as though she had the initials JP on her neck. She also felt that this "was not a room for woman."

All guests were now feeling uneasy and some were complaining of feeling nauseous. Two other guests said that around this room there was the name of Thomas M and the date of 1827, though she could not be sure if this was related to the Scotsman or the room itself. Paul felt once again that this room also had layers of history within it, as described in other parts of the hall, as though it has been built on the site of a previous building, or bricks/stone from that previous building had been used in the construction of a new building. One other aspect that Paul had not mentioned during this vigil was that he felt he was backlit, as though a light was shining from behind him. But as the images and sensations were fading from the room a guest commented that he has felt there was a bright light shining from behind Paul, lighting him up from his knees to his head. What this was or if it had any significance Paul did not know and others could not add to either. All the guests were glad to step out of the atmosphere of the room and most wanted a break to get a drink and a chance to clear their minds and the emotions. So a 15-minute break was taken and the rest of the party was joined back in the base room.

IRON DOOR ROOM

That maybe on odd way to describe a room but it is the most accurate. Opposite the base room was a larger room that was striking by the large and heavy iron door that was its entry point. Due to the surface rust on this door and the absence of any bright lights at first glance it could easily be taken as streaks of blood. However guests were asked to ignore that image if possible and just treat it as a normal room. During the course of the night several differing groups of varying amounts of people had spent time in this room. Some had undertaken solo vigils and the less brave had gone in as pairs. All had encountered activity or sights of varying degrees and sorts, often they were sights of a similar nature but at times they differed wildly.

So after the break was completed it was agreed to hold a séance in the room as the final event of the night. During this séance it was to be the entire group who took part except Stephen who simply wanted to stand back and observe and possibly take pictures if something interesting was apparent. This is a particularly useful way of recording a séance as it allows someone not wrapped up in the emotions of the circle to be an impartial observer. Prior to this particular séance there had been as said differing types of activities experienced in this room. All of the groups had seen what was described as bubbles looking like those in lemonade that form and pop in the liquid. But in this instance they formed in the air and were much brighter, one person describing them as "glowing." Interestingly each differing group saw this only in one part of the room and each group reported that to Paul and Stephen independently of the other groups.

One group had a very interesting experience. They had seen a light seeming to shine through the gaps between the door and the frame. It seemed that this light was coming from low down and was not as bright or direct as a torch beam. As the light grew brighter and neared, the group started to hear what seemed to be footsteps in the corridor outside approaching the door. It was doubtful if this was any other member of another party as they group had split into two and the other party was at a location on the other side of the estate. As the steps grew nearer and passed the room one of the guests quickly strode over to the door and heaved it open. There was nothing outside and there were no obvious light sources that could explain the light, let alone the footsteps.

That group were eager to see if once the rest of the team returned to see if their return could replicate the effects of a light as they had seen. Again this was simply to rule out another possible logical reason for the anomaly. But despite many attempts they could not get the same effect. They tried everything from walking up and down the corridor with torches held at varying angles, to shining torches through the gaps and blank windows at the front of the building. However, they could not achieve an effect that was even close to the images they had seen.

So the entire group settled into the chairs that had been placed in the room, the door was closed and as usual Paul asked everyone to spend 10 minutes letting their eyes adjust to the darkness and to calm their minds. After that had elapsed Paul asked for any of the group to voice anything they could see, hear or feel in this room. There were various different reports coming from the group. Many reporting, seeing or sensing a family group in the same area that others had reported seeing the "lemonade" lights. One other guest reported seeing a large table in the centre of the room. The table was described as a "Butchers table with a central part that things were placed on and other shallow cubby holes set into the top of the surface of the table." The reason for this table and what the cubbyholes were for was not obvious and to date no reason is known for this type of table.

As it seemed that there was a lull in the activities in the room Paul began to ask out to any energies present. Readers who have read other chapters will understand this method of encouraging paranormal activity. Despite several attempts and the fact Paul could sense the man Gregory hovering in the corridor there was no further significant activity. Two guests did say they thought they heard faint footsteps in the corridor outside as though someone was there but attempting to hide their presence. As 3 am, the time for the end of the event, was approaching Paul started to close the circle down. As usual he asked for torches to be lit so he could check everyone was fine and fully alert. At that point Paul became aware that one of the guests, John appeared to be having breathing problems. Observing him for a few seconds Paul was aware that this was not a physical manifestation of any illness but an attempt by a spirit to make contact. Occasionally spirit energy will choose to try and use the body of a medium to communicate. This is commonly known as trance mediumship and is a form of mediumship not that common on such events. As a rule it is the mental style of mediumship rather than the physical that is the most common.

As John was an experienced medium Paul was not too concerned, he would have been if this had occurred to anyone who was not a medium. He continued to observe him closely though and after some time it seemed there was an impasse. The spirit energy was not making his presence felt any further but neither was John's personality returning to the fore. Paul asked that one of Johns friends to speak to him; he felt a familiar voice would help. However there was little response to

206

this and as Johns hands began to shake and his breathing continued to be harsh and shallow. Paul decided take further action. As a rule it is not considered normal practise to break a circle while the medium was in trance. However Paul became increasingly sure that this was needed. Not wanting to fully break the circle Paul instead stood and changed his position within the circle so he was closer to John. After a few more minutes John drew a deep and gasping lungful of air and started to regain awareness of his surroundings. As he recovered he told that he felt there was a man who had at first wanted to come through to the group but he "was afraid that he would be judged." Why or what he was afraid of or what he was to be judged on was not apparent. It did take several minutes for John to regain his usual personality and at times though, being as a rule a fairly mild and gentle man he displayed some flashes of anger and resentment. So Paul was at pains to ensure that John was fully recovered before everyone left the room and the guests were allowed to head home. After about 15 minutes it seemed everything and everyone was fine so possessions were gathered and good byes were said. As they were all heading towards the cars Paul and Stephen again reminded all the guests to be cautious when leaving.

As mentioned the exit was back along a narrow track with a drainage ditch on one side. Most of the guests managed to reverse up the pitch-black lane with the assistance of a torch shone by Stephen but one ended up in the ditch. Of course it was the last car to leave so there was only Paul and Stephen left to help get it out. After a bit of effort the car was at last free and Paul and Stephen were covered in mud. However before this chapter is closed there is still the last little bits of information gathered by guests. Some was gained in the area over the stile mentioned earlier in the chapter. Due to there being several days of heavy rain leading up to the weekend this area was very boggy. At one point Paul sank shin deep in mud. However some guests felt that this area had at one point been the main access point to the estate, though it did not at this time look like a road at all. Some guests also complained of feeling unsafe, as though they had been plotted against and were being watched. Lastly there was a little bit of random information picked up by some guests. That being the names Burtrum, Bartrum and Bartholomew associated with the site with the dates of "circa1660."

Paul and Stephen will return to this site as it is felt there are still facts to uncover. Let's just hope that next time the mud has disappeared and no one finds the ditch again.

A Witch's Guide To Sexuality & Good Relationships By Tarona Hawkins & Howard Rodway
ISBN 978-1-906958-14-5, £11.99

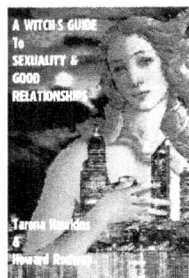

Four years ago when I was discussing the subject of natural healing with practising witch Dr Tarona Hawkins, she mentioned during our conversation that she had notes, files and first draft chapters prepared about her psychic readings, counselling, past life regression work, magickal treatments and herbal remedies, all relating to clients' sexual problems.

Tarona Hawkins added that her reputation as a sex witch had gathered such momentum that most of her time was now occupied with sex counselling. This volume is the end result of accepting Tarona's invitation to transform her records and her knowledge into *A WITCH'S GUIDE to SEXUALITY and GOOD RELATIONSHIPS*.

Within this book you will find covered an incredible variety of sex and sex related subjects, for example: Sex magick, sex massage, adult babies, fetishism, demonic sexual encounters, group sex, homosexuality, anal sex, sadomasochism, transvestism, transsexualism, sex feeders, sex for the elderly, impotence, penis enlargement, male hygiene, menstruation, past life traumas, the human sexual aura, sexual handwriting characteristics together with other sex related subjects.

To all those who read this book; individual members of the public, those with sexual problems, sex counsellors, and of course the occult community, it is hoped that through this book new insights will be gained into the unusually varied spectrum of human sexual behaviour.

Order direct from
Mandrake of Oxford, PO Box 250, Oxford, OX1 1AP (UK)
Phone: 01865 243671 (for credit card sales)
Prices include economy postage
online at - www.mandrake.uk.net

Lightning Source UK Ltd.
Milton Keynes UK
UKOW06f1019160317
296758UK00008B/141/P